AGAINST THE GRAIN

AGAINST THE GRAIN

Raising Christ-Focused Children
from A to Z

Dr. Michele White

New York

AGAINST THE GRAIN

Raising Christ-Focused Children from A to Z

© 2017 Dr. Michele White.

Published in New York, New York, by Morgan James Publishing. Morgan James and The Entrepreneurial Publisher are trademarks of Morgan James, LLC. www.MorganJamesPublishing.com

The Morgan James Speakers Group can bring authors to your live event. For more information or to book an event visit The Morgan James Speakers Group at www.TheMorganJamesSpeakersGroup.com.

Shelfie

A free eBook edition is available with the purchase of this print book.

CLEARLY PRINT YOUR NAME ABOVE IN UPPER CASE

Instructions to claim your free eBook edition:
1. Download the Shelfie app for Android or iOS
2. Write your name in **UPPER CASE** above
3. Use the Shelfie app to submit a photo
4. Download your eBook to any device

ISBN 978-1-63047-957-2 paperback
ISBN 978-1-63047-959-6 eBook
ISBN 978-1-63047-958-9 hardcover
Library of Congress Control Number:
2016901011

Cover Design by:
Rachel Lopez
www.r2cdesign.com

Interior Design by:
Bonnie Bushman
The Whole Caboodle Graphic Design

In an effort to support local communities and raise awareness and funds, Morgan James Publishing donates a percentage of all book sales for the life of each book to Habitat for Humanity Peninsula and Greater Williamsburg.

Get involved today, visit
www.MorganJamesBuilds.com

Habitat for Humanity®
Peninsula and
Greater Williamsburg
Building Partner

This book is dedicated to my wonderful husband,
Paul Dewaune White,
and our five beautiful children,
Alexia, Alonzo, Alyssa, Avery and Autumn.

CONTENTS

ACKNOWLEDGEMENTS

I cannot possibly thank and acknowledge each and every person who has contributed to this book through prayer and support. The pages would exceed the length of the book. I am eternally grateful for the love, support, constant prayers, and pep talks from all of my family and friends across the country.

However, I would be remiss if I did not take a moment and share my heart's gratitude to a few people, without whom, I may be still wondering if I should write this book.

My first acknowledgement must be my Lord and Savior Jesus Christ. I am completely unashamed of the Gospel of Jesus Christ and proclaim Him Lord over my life. Without Him, there would be no book. Thank you Lord!

Thank you to my wonderful husband Paul. I love sharing life with you and am humbled that God gave you to me. You have been my constant cheerleader, coach, prayer warrior and confidante through this entire process. You always believe in me before I believe in myself. Your constant encouragement is amazing. Thank you for being such a Godly example of love and being our head.

Thank you, my beautiful children, Alexia, Alonzo, Alyssa, Avery and Autumn. Without you, I would not be a mother and be passionate about helping other parents discover how to raise Christ-focused children. I am honored and humbled to be a mom to such great kids. Thank you for being an awesome blessing.

Although my beautiful grandmother, Georgia Mae Virginia Alston, died in 2009, her impact is still felt in my life daily. I am so grateful that she led me to Jesus Christ in my teen years and showed me how to live as a Christian.

Thank you to my best friend Kenyatta Stephens. I am amazed at how you always knew the exact moment when to pray during the course of writing this book. Your constant words of encouragement kept me focused on God's plan. Thank you for being an amazing woman of God.

Thank you to my awesome friend Cheryl McKinney. Without you, how would this book ever been completed? Thank you for the countless hours that you spent editing, proofing, correcting, transcribing, and reading the manuscript. Your unselfish and constant love for God is so apparent in all you touch.

Thank you to my loving parents, Matthew and Lydia Alston. I appreciate that you always believe that I can do the impossible. Thank you for the many sacrifices that you made to allow me to achieve my dreams. I could never say thank you enough.

Thank you to my loving in-laws, Paul and Carolynne White. You have always been a wonderful example to me of how to raise Christ-focused children. I am truly grateful.

Thank you to my siblings, my brother Matthew John Alston, my sister, and brother-in-law Lucius White. I appreciate your love and willingness to listen and be proud of everything that I do. I love you dearly and thank God for your presence in my life. And to my sister, thank you for volunteering to read my manuscript and offer sound marketing advice. Thank you for being a blessing.

Thank you to all of my family members spread across the country who prayed and supported me during the writing of this book. Thank you to the Bogees, Parks, Wyatts, Parhams, Joneses, Walkers, Campbells, Whites, and my Middlebelt Baptist Church family.

Thank you to the entire team at Morgan James Publishing for selecting this book to be a part of your family.

PREFACE

As I peer across the crowded restaurant, my eyes become fixed on the number of families with children. Some of the children are laughing, some are playing, some are crying, and some are even arguing. I begin to ponder what makes each child laugh, play, cry, or argue.

I continue to pan across the restaurant when my eyes briefly stop and lock eyes with an elderly woman. We immediately exchange a cordial smile, and I resume my inspection of the restaurant.

Suddenly, my six-year-old breaks my gaze with a question. As I'm engaged with her, I notice through my peripheral vision the elderly woman that I exchanged a cordial smile with approach our table. She looks at both my husband and myself and says, "Your children are so well behaved. You have great children. Are all five of these children yours?" My husband and I smile, and we both answer, "Thank you. Yes, all five children are ours."

We are asked many times, what is our secret to having well behaved children. After we give honor to God for their behavior, we answer very simply. Our answer often is that our children are just like any other child that God has given into any family; however, we spend dedicated time pouring individually into each one. This makes a difference. We have chosen a path that aligns with God's Word and allows us to focus our energy on raising Christ-focused children as opposed to children that conform to the world.

I am the first to admit that we are not a perfect family. We have the tantrums. We have the fights. We have the disobedience. We have all of the things that make parents drop to their knees in prayer. We have decided to go against the grain. This terminology, "against the grain," is a very fascinating one to me. I heard this terminology once in a sermon at my church. My pastor talked about Christians needing to have the mentality of going against what the world says is acceptable and choosing a path that is totally different.

My husband and I subscribe to Ecclesiastes 4:9–12 in many areas of our lives. We are quickly reminded that God's Word calls us to be united as husband and wife only as we are utilizing the thread that binds us, which is God. God allows the threefold cord to not quickly be broken. Although this is a book on parenting, I must emphasize one point. If the relationship between the husband and wife is not based in God, nothing that they can do as parents will produce the fruit that will allow their children to be Christ-focused.

This book has been a remarkable journey of an 18-year desire. Eighteen years ago when we had our first child we knew absolutely nothing about parenting. Let me stop for a moment and add that I do not have every single answer 18 years and five children later. What I do have is a strong love for the Lord and desire to obey His calling to write this book. I am excited to share what He has shown me during my journey as a mother.

Why should you read this book? It's different than most that you will find. I am a counselor and behavioral psychologist who loves being the mother of five children. My goal is to share encouragement as a mother of five, biblical knowledge as a Christian, and clinical knowledge as a professional dealing with behavioral issues.

The format of the book is quite simple. My desire is to have a book that is timeless. Each letter of the alphabet delineates every chapter. The book can be read from A to Z, or in any given order depending upon the life stage that you may be in with your children. By timeless, I mean that you can re-read a chapter based on your current life stage.

Every chapter will have a very similar format. I will start with a scripture that will relate to the subject matter of the chapter. I will examine the principle or concept based on a world perspective. Then, by infusing encouragement as a mother, biblical understanding, and professional knowledge, I will connect the pieces to produce a practical application.

Then at the end of every chapter you will have a takeaway that will give you specific instructions on how to implement the principle within your home. Have you ever enjoyed making words out of alphabet soup? Each letter links together and becomes your story. As you read each chapter, the concepts will link together and create your family story. Therefore, the takeaway section at the end of each chapter will be labeled alphabet soup.

There is so much laughter within our home that it is my joy to share several of our journeys with you. This is a smaller paperback, and thus you will not be able to fully enjoy each and every journey that we have had with our children over 18 years. I guess that means you'll have to buy subsequent books to continue the journey with us.

Prior to starting our journey together, allow me to share a little bit about who we are. God has blessed me with an amazing husband, whose name is Paul. He is my best friend and confidante. He leads our home according to God's voice. We have security in knowing his submission to God directs our home. We have been married for almost 23 years, as of the date of this book. Our union has brought forth five children. Our oldest is Alexia, age 18. Alexia is a gifted musician who graduated from high school in 2015. She was the homecoming queen and valedictorian of her senior class. She has dedicated her life to serving Christ and continuing her education within a Christian university, Calvin College.

After Alexia, we were then blessed to have twins, Alonzo and Alyssa. As of the date of this book they are 13. Alonzo is a very compassionate, loving child, who plays basketball and is very bright in all that he does. Alyssa is an entrepreneur who crochets, knits, sews, and has a true servant's heart. Both have committed their life to Christ at the age of around seven.

Our house was not loud enough, or busy enough, so God decided to give us a little pizazz. God added our fourth child, Avery. He is a wonderful firecracker and is 10 years old. He is the most loving child and academically astute in the subjects that he pursues. God has given him a strong passion for soccer. He breathes, eats, lives and dreams all things soccer. He also has made a profession of faith at an early age and serves Christ and understands the tenants of His word as best he can from a ten year old perspective.

Again God realized that there was still something missing at the White house, so He decided to put a sweet topping on top of our house. God gave us little Autumn. She is seven years old. She is a compassionate, loving, vivacious little girl. She is all things girl. Her mind is very inquisitive when it comes to understanding the relationship that she has with Christ. She asks many questions daily about God. Jeremiah 29:13 reminds us that as we seek God, we will find Him. I am happy to say that Autumn did just that. She accepted Jesus Christ as her personal Lord and Savior in 2015. Like the Apostle Paul, she is truly unashamed of the Gospel of Jesus Christ.

I am overjoyed that all five children have been able to be educated within a Christian setting. All five have attended Washtenaw Christian Academy for several years. Classical Christian education has given them a true complement to the foundation that has been built upon at home and church.

Lastly, the most important person that I want to introduce you to is my Lord and Savior, Jesus Christ. John 3:16 says, "For God so loved the world that He gave His only begotten Son, that whoever believes in Him should not perish but have everlasting life." Jesus died on the cross for our sins. In order to benefit fully from this book, you need to know Him for yourself. If you do not remember a time in your life that you asked Jesus into your heart to be your Lord and Savior, today can be that day. Just like my book, it is as easy as ABC:

A—ADMIT that you are a sinner in need of salvation (Romans 3:23), that you deserve to die (Romans 6:23), that one day you will be judged by the Lord (Hebrews 9:27), and that you cannot save yourself by good works (Titus 3:5).

B—BELIEVE the facts of the gospel. The Lord Jesus Christ, the Son of God, died for our sins on the cross and He rose again from the dead. He is the Savior of those who believe in Him (Romans 5:8; John 3:16, 36)

C—CONFESS and CALL upon the Lord. Confess with your mouth that Jesus is Lord and believe in your heart that God raised Him from the dead and you will be saved. Ask Jesus to come into your heart right now (Psalm 145:18; Romans 10:13; Romans 10:9).

Your family will thank you!!!!!

Let's begin our journey. Happy reading.

Chapter **A**

AFFIRMATION

EPHESIANS 4:29—*Do not let any unwholesome talk come out of your mouths, but only what is helpful for building others up according to their needs, that it may benefit those who listen.*

I t is interesting that the word "affirmation" sometimes is looked at as a negative thing. Many individuals feel that affirmation needs to come from an internal place as opposed to an external person.

One day I was teaching at Wayne State University and several students indicated that they were school teachers within a local school system. All of the teachers indicated that during their orientation they were told that there is a new teaching method that forbids them from affirming their students. Being puzzled, I questioned a little more of what they meant. They indicated that the new teaching method wants students to find internal gratification as opposed to external gratification.

For example, if a kindergartener draws a picture, the teacher is not allowed to say the picture is beautiful. The reasoning behind this is that every time the child draws a picture the child will seek gratification from that one person and want to please that one person as opposed to knowing that their work is intrinsically good and they can create it on their own. I asked each of the teachers in the class that day, what is then the appropriate response to a beautiful picture drawn by a five-year-old? They indicated that the appropriate response would be to tell the child to work at creating another picture that looks just like this one, or create a different type of picture using different materials.

Although the conversation ceased that day, it has put a permanent imprint in my mind of where society has taken such a wrong turn. We are so focused on being politically correct that we are not Biblically correct. God's Word tells us to edify one another. God's Word instructs us to build one another up. In the building up of one another, the most precious little people that God has given to us to build up are our children. It is imperative that we see the error of not affirming our children.

I have been able to understand this concept just watching my own five children flourish in different areas of their self-esteem. My children truly believe that they can accomplish anything. It is not solely based on an academic aptitude or sports ability or some type of external ability that they think that they may have. It is based on God giving us, as parents, the ability to affirm them and to reach and touch a part of them that longs for edification.

Amazingly, affirmation can have such a positive impact when it comes to relationship issues with your children. Let me explain. I remember when our oldest daughter was in middle school and she was approached by young boys that wanted to be her boyfriend. They would attempt to give her gifts, or they would attempt to give her cards. My daughter has been told from birth how beautiful she is and how she does not need to be affirmed by a boy. We have stressed to her that she could stand strong on who God has made her and understand that the earthly parents that her heavenly Father has given to her can provide for her needs more so than any young boy. By continuing to affirm that within her, she was able to deny those gifts and not feel that she was missing out on anything.

I have to be honest, that it was not always an easy discussion initially with her, because who wouldn't want a little boy giving you a beautiful card with money in it for your birthday. I still remember the look on her face when her father told her she had to go back to school and give the money back to the little boy, but she could keep the card, and she had to explain why. I saw that process with her and her father as being such a wonderful growth opportunity, that he affirmed who she is as a young woman growing in Christ. It was such a turning point for her because then she understood that she couldn't be bought by someone, but she could choose to have relationships with those individuals that she chooses without feeling that they have to buy her affection because she was strong enough within herself.

From a clinical standpoint, 90 percent of the individuals that will come into therapy with me will struggle with the issue of low self-esteem. Often I use a psychodynamic approach with them, which means going back into their familial history to truly figure out how their family history has impacted them today. I find that many of them were never affirmed as a child. They were never affirmed in the home. They were never affirmed in their schools. And their church assumed that they were being affirmed in the home or school and therefore attempted to come alongside in some cases, but that affirmation, because it never started at home, never took root.

Understand the concept of what I just said with a visual picture of a tree. The parent roots the child based upon this concept of affirmation. Affirmation becomes part of the planting process to establish secure roots. As we look at affirmation as taking root into the ground, you have built such a strong foundation for them that they can weather many storms as they come their way because they have been affirmed.

As I work with these individuals who struggle with self-esteem issues, we first seek God's word. We find so many wonderful passages where God affirms them as His children, where God reminds them that He has created them in His own image. God reminds them that even before the earth was formed He knew every hair that was going to be placed on their head; that this is a picture of a loving Father who took His time to create them and knew them and loved them before they were even here. Once an individual has been affirmed in God, it's much like the analogy that I gave with the tree; that once they know that affirmation from God those roots take place and they will be able to weather the storms that come into their lives.

Another issue that sometimes plagues many families is favoritism. I have had several parents ask how I equally affirm my children without being partial to others. I remember growing up hearing the words, "This child is my favorite," or "I like you better." The children that are close by hearing a parent use these words will then begin to understand that if one child is their favorite, then that means they are not. What a powerful message that sends to a young child, to hear that they are not the apple of their parent's eye.

So to answer the question, how do you equally affirm your children, you speak highly of each of them in front of each of them, in front of others, in front of the world. I laugh with my children because I tell each of them how they, at whatever given moment of their age, are my favorite. What I mean by that, and it's not contradicting what I just said, is that I will say to my seven-year-old daughter, that she is my absolute favorite seven-year-old daughter ever. At seven, she still thinks that is absolutely wonderful and special. She will smile and I will see a glow as she just runs down the hallway yelling, "I am mommy's favorite seven-year-old."

Now, my 13-year-old twins, when I tell them that they are my absolute favorite 13-year-old twins ever, they both look at me with a grin and say, "Mommy, we're your only 13-year-old twins." Then I reply, "Nonetheless, you're still my favorite 13-year-old twins." My children expect that type of silly affirmation from me because it is true. At whatever age they are, I love them equally, and they need to understand that. To ever say that a child is a favorite over another is damaging to the entire familial structure of the home, because then envy, rivalry, and all of those things that naturally come into a home without any effort, multiply and grow.

A B C
ALPHABET SOUP

1. Take time with your child on a daily basis to find something that is good in their environment that they have done. Many times as parents we are so quick to correct and to discipline our children and forget to affirm. There is definitely a time and place for discipline and to have some time of correction based on their behavior; however, it needs to be coupled daily with finding things that are positive about your child. Therefore, I want to encourage you today to make a list of the things that "wow" you about your child and give that list to your child. Maybe you will frame it, maybe you could put it on a bulletin board, but every time that child has a doubt about the world around them they can look at that piece of paper and remember that I have been affirmed, first and foremost by my heavenly

Father, and then secondly by the earthly parents that have been given to me.

2. Have a family meeting. During the family meeting have siblings affirm each other. Have the siblings say one positive thing that they like about their sibling, and then tell them how much they appreciate the things that they do to make the family a family. These are wonderful ways that you can begin to affirm your child just like your Father in heaven has affirmed you.

Chapter B

BIBLE

2 TIMOTHY 3:16—*All scripture is God-breathed and is useful for teaching, rebuking, correcting and training in righteousness.*

According to Guinness World Records,[1] the Bible is the best-selling book of all time, with over 5 billion copies sold and distributed. With these amazing numbers, it amazes me that our society still tends to discount much of what is written in the Bible.

I once heard a pastor say that we treat the Bible like a buffet table; we only take what we want and leave the rest on the table. This is so incredibly true. The problem with this is, 2 Timothy 3:16 states that all scripture is given by God; therefore, if He gave "all" scripture, then it is imperative for us to follow "all" scripture. Unfortunately, we as parents oftentimes live our lives in a partial following, and we do this in front of our children. Then when we attempt to teach our children to follow what God's word says we are then deemed as hypocrites because we are not following what God's word says.

7

This leads to a whole other issue: How can we follow what God's word says if there's a lack of knowledge of what the Bible says? If you're reading this book, whether you are a new Christian or a mature Christian, do not despair if you feel that you do not know everything that's in the Bible. My statements are not to make anyone feel inadequate, but my statements are used to edify you in the body of Christ to seek out more. We each have the ability to go into God's word and search and dig for answers that will help our families. When we don't know, God says to ask. Stop and pray before reading His word and ask him to open your ears and heart to digest and understand His word. I pray that is the reason that you are reading this book, because you're interested in digging and finding out more answers.

As I stated earlier, the Bible cannot be used like a buffet table. I often wonder if we do that in our humanness because we don't want to be confronted with what our sin may look like in the light, or we truly don't know how to find the answers because God's Bible is so overwhelming. I remember being a new Christian and thinking that there are so many things in here that I don't know and that I will never measure up to the person who is a biblical scholar. But God quickly changed my heart and mind to understand that if my eyes are fixed on Him, He will guide me to the passages, He will guide me to where He wants me to read, and He will guide me to understanding.

I began to be so hungry for God's word, that just looking within the text wasn't enough. I needed a study Bible that would take me deep into the history, deep into the back story of each of the wonderful individuals that walked during biblical times. I began to have a quest to find out why certain things happened. God continued to grow me in faith and grow me in knowledge based upon my sitting at His feet. There was no syringe that went into an I.V. that infused my body with the knowledge. I think that's a misconception, that people will see those who are biblical scholars, as they call them, or call themselves, and assume that this knowledge was just truly, through intravenous method, given to this person.

I'm here to tell you as a witness of God's unending grace that that is not the case. I spent years at His feet, and I still spend time at His feet now, because I don't know everything that's in the Bible. I don't know everything that God would have for me and I don't understand everything. But what I'm grateful for is that I am so much further in my journey as a Christian than I once was. I continue to make strides towards where God would have me to be.

I have a question for you. How often do your children see you reading the Bible? It's harder today to really answer that question because of all the electronic methods that we have in order to access the Bible. I know for myself, I'm a techie geek and my Bible is on my iPad, and so very often when I am in scripture and looking at certain things I'm reading my Bible on my iPad. So traditionally, when you would see a parent sitting with an actual leather-bound Bible in their hand, the child would understand that the parent is now sitting at Jesus' feet reading, learning and gleaning. Now you can't tell if they are in their Bible or if they're playing Angry Birds. Therefore, I would recommend that you share with your child, when you're reading your Bible on your iPad, something that God has spoken to you in that moment.

This book is written to address all age groups, and so as you are looking at a kindergartener, a preschooler, an infant, a teenager, a young adult, you could still use the same exact principle to be able to do that. You can share with a kindergartener what you just read in God's word and summarize it for them and make it so real to them. Never underestimate the power that God's word has with every single age group.

Once I was speaking in the south and I had a lovely conversation with an older woman. She and I talked about how we just love the Bible, and she talked about how she uses it everywhere she goes. And that was a very interesting way of putting it, that she uses it everywhere she goes. So then I began to think of an analogy of a vehicle. Think about your vehicle, and think about what's in your glove compartment. Every single vehicle has an owner's manual, typically in their glove compartment. That owner's manual is your key to understanding every single thing there is to know about your vehicle. Sometimes it can be a little overwhelming, because it can be 300 pages, it seems. You may be trying to figure out how to turn the automatic lights off, and you have to go through so many sections to find that one little piece of information.

God's word is exactly the same. The Bible is your instruction manual for your life. It is your owner's manual to know exactly what to do in every single circumstance. If you're broken down on the side of the road, you can go to God's Word. If you're having trouble in your marriage, you can go to God's Word. If you are struggling with an addiction, you can go to God's Word. If you're struggling with wayward children, you can go to God's Word. If you're struggling with anything in your life, you can go to God's Word.

Also, when you're happy, you can go to God's Word. When you're joyful about things that have happened in the lives of others, you can go to God's Word. The Bible is there for you to utilize every single day.

Have you heard the statement that anything that you do for 28 days becomes a habit? Try that with your Bible. Try being habitual with reading and learning your Bible. I love the fact that God's word even tells us, that if we don't understand, read and He will open our eyes and ears to what He is saying amongst the beautiful pages that He has given us.

Let your children see the love that you have and the value that you give to God's Word. I remember when my twins were about five or six years old and my husband had left home for the day and left his Bible sitting on the kitchen table. One of the twins began to sob. And I walked over to him and I said, "Alonzo, what's wrong?" He said, "Daddy's going to get arrested." And I said, "Why do you say that he's going to get arrested?" He said, "Because he never leaves without his Bible, and he left his Bible, and the police will tell him you're not supposed to leave without your Bible."

That truly warmed my heart, to hear him understand the importance of God's Word within our home and know that his dad left his Bible, and that that is an important piece of who his father is. Of course, I had to explain that the police were not going to come get daddy; that it's okay daddy left the Bible today, he will come back tonight and read it. That put a smile back on his face and we went on about your day.

A B C
ALPHABET SOUP

1. Read, read, read, to yourself and to your children. It is imperative that they see the connection that you have to your Bible and to God. You cannot read alone and expect to have an impact on your children. When your children are asked the question in school, what is your parents' favorite book, they should immediately be able to know the answer is the Bible. It should not be something that is of the world; it should be something that you have rooted yourself in as a family. Depending on the age of your child, read with your child.

2. Have family discussion around the dinner table about certain Bible stories.

3. Another fun activity is, at the dinner table play Bible trivia. There are a lot of Bible trivia games that you can find on Amazon that you could play while you're eating. You could have your children be on teams and they can race to see who gets the correct answer first. There are some games that you can find in

different Christian bookstores that would allow you to have the children race to look up certain things.

4. You do not always have to go to a Christian bookstore or to Amazon to find something that will be impactful for your family. Try just using the Bible. Have Bible races after dinner, on a Saturday morning, Sunday after church; whatever your time frame may be, ask your children to race and look up a certain verse and then stand up and read it. And you can give out prizes, or you can give out special accolades to the person who is able to find it the fastest.

The Bible needs to be a cornerstone and a foundation for your home. Use it to God's glory.

Chapter C

CULTIVATE

PROVERBS 22:6—*Train up a child in the way he should go, and when he is old he will not depart from it.*

hat images are conjured in your mind when you think of a crisp fall morning? For our family, that answer is quite easy. We think of soccer. Our fourth child, Avery, is an avid soccer player. He loves all things soccer. Our goal is to help cultivate this love, while balancing it with the right priorities.

The definition of the word "cultivate" means to try to acquire or develop. What does that look like from the worldview lens? From a worldview lens, sometimes we see an overstimulation as a way to cultivate a talent or a love for a child. We see the following terms: "helicopter parent," "tiger mom," or "stage mom." All of these depict a parent that has taken a love or a talent to the extreme. Instead of helping to truly cultivate something that would be positive, some parents will turn that cultivating process into a negative experience. This can cause a child to dislike being a part of an organized sport or an activity.

When I think of the word "cultivate," I am reminded that we are called to cultivate a relationship with Christ above all other relationships. It is imperative that our children develop a relationship with Christ separate from our relationship. I hear many times, young people say that they know that they're saved based on the fact that their parents were saved or their grandparents went to church. The truth is, they're not saved based on those facts. Each individual, whether it's an adult or a child, has an individual relationship with Christ that needs to be cultivated.

Allow me to share an analogy. Using analogies is one of my favorite teaching modalities. I think about how Jesus used parables to bring forth truth in a way that is digestible by all. I think of analogies in the same way.

If you think of the analogy of being in a grocery store and there is a lost child running wild in the store; the child is running wild because they are fearful that they have lost their parent, so they begin to scream, "Mom, mom, mom." Despite the number of children that are running around that store, a mother can hear the voice of her child no matter all other external noises. Their voice may be faint, but a mother can hone in on the intricate details and nuances of that child's voice unlike any other mother. In fact, there could be a hundred other mothers that go by the name of mom, but your mom knows your voice.

The same is exactly true with a relationship with Jesus Christ. When you make a profession of faith to become part of a parent-child relationship unlike any other, God, being your Father, hears your voice. He hears the nuances and intricacies of your voice unlike any other child; as you run aimlessly around the world He hears your unique voice. What a joy to be able to share with your child this concept of cultivating.

Much like the relationship that you teach your child within your home about cultivating a relationship with Jesus Christ, you must understand that you as a parent must cultivate a relationship with your child. Many times we err on the side of trying to put activities in place of the relationship. We think that if we take them to a thousand soccer practices or a thousand violin lessons or a million piano lessons, that this will bring joy and it will cause that child to see us as a super parent.

Out of every single gift that my parents have ever bestowed upon me as a child, the one that I remember most is the gift of time. I remember times of mowing the grass with my father. I remember times of driving to school with my mother and the conversations that we would have during my senior year of high school. Of course I remember a few of the gifts that were given to me for birthdays and Christmases, but they pale in comparison to the gift of time.

We fill our time, unfortunately, with items as opposed to relationships. I implore you to sit down with your child and cultivate a close relationship with them that is not based on activity, but is based on you understanding who they are. I don't want to give the wrong impression, that events and items of interest to your child are not important; however, there has to be a proper balance.

With our son Avery, we are very structured in our time and he understands that although soccer is a priority in his life, it is not a priority in our family structure, or in God's kingdom. We also implore upon our son that God will use his talents and He will use different events on the soccer field to first and foremost bring glory to God. As we begin to teach Avery how to cultivate both, this relationship with us and with God, his soccer skills and soccer love come naturally. Therefore, his "loves" are properly ordered. He understands that his love for God is first, his love for parents is second, his love for his siblings is next, and then love for soccer falls after extended family.

In the book of Matthew, God encourages us, "To seek ye first the kingdom of God." If we teach our children to seek God first, then God, according to His word, will order everything else in proper succession. We have been able to see the fruit of this with each one of our children as we begin to prioritize those things that are most important in our family structure.

Having five children, they each have a different personality and each have a different bent. God has given them each a unique gift and a unique talent that will be utilized in God's kingdom. Ultimately, God will have us give an account of how we best used our gifts and talents. We understand, with soccer being a gift, that soccer will be used at some point for our son to spread God's Word. He is able to do that while on the soccer field by showing Christ-like love when there's an injury, showing compassion for a teammate. He's able to show Christ-like love when there are decisions that are made that he may not agree with by speaking to the referee with respect. He is able to continue to edify God by saying no to a game that may interfere with church or family activities.

Our children understand that the world does not dictate and run our home, but rather, God does. Every decision that my husband and I make within our home comes through thoughtful prayer and consideration of how that aligns with God's Word. In order to raise a Christ-focused child, it must begin with Christ. Part of the reason for doing a book about Christ-focused children is to make sure that we as parents understand the significance of Christ being the center of everything.

If Christ is truly the anchor that holds everything down, our children will be able to handle the extracurricular activities in a manner that will be pleasing to God our Father, to our family, and to the entity in which they belong.

A B C
ALPHABET SOUP

1. Sit down with your child every two weeks for a parent-child date night. I would encourage you to schedule on your calendar a time every two weeks that you can spend uninterrupted time with your child. This does not have to be a time where you go out, but just a time to talk with them and cultivate your relationship.

2. It is imperative that you begin with prayer with your child and have a fervent prayer life with them to hear their heart. It is also imperative that you know what their likes and what their desires are and what their fears are. Have a conversation about school. Have a conversation about social relationships. As you begin to cultivate a relationship with your child you will understand that your child will not have a fear of coming to you to discuss any matter.

I laugh at the thought that my 18-year-old shares more things with me than I may be ready as a parent to hear, but I am humbled by the fact that God allowed me to cultivate such a precious relationship with her early on that she feels comfortable sharing the delicate details of her heart.

Be encouraged on this day, that cultivating a relationship with your child can bring amazing results.

Chapter D

DISCIPLINE

PROVERBS 13:24—*He who spares his rod hates his son, but he who loves him disciplines him promptly.*

I am almost 50 years old and can remember vividly how I was disciplined as a child. Unlike my younger sister, who was only spanked once in her life, I cannot tell you how many times my parents adhered to Proverbs 13:24 in relation to me. Let's just say they really loved me.

ABC News conducted a nationwide survey in October 2015 with approximately 1100 parents. There were two questions asked. The first question asked was, "Do you approve of spanking a child?" The second question asked was, "Do you spank your child?" Sixty-five percent of those asked indicated that they approve of spanking. This number has held steady since 1990. Interestingly, only 45 to 50 percent actually spank their children, and indicated even this was occasionally.

Another interesting tidbit was that the percentages changed depending on the demographics. Depending upon where the poll was taken, in what part of the country, the percentages were either higher or lower. For instance, 75 percent of those polled in the south indicated that they approve of spanking their children. I find this fascinating because that area of the country is commonly known as the Bible belt. I was actually surprised by the number given in the poll.

Based on what I see in my daily personal and professional realm, I don't see discipline being used as often as this poll indicated. Let me elaborate. The word "discipline" is defined as the practice of training people to obey rules or a code of behavior. Training takes patience and time. Since we live in such a microwave generation, we want to quickly address everything and move on. Therefore, oftentimes I see a parent bartering with a child to behave appropriately, or utilizing a "time-out" system to allow the child to have space and to reflect.

A parent should never have to barter with a child to behave. There should be clear expectations of what appropriate behavior entails and there should be accountability to follow the correct behavior regardless of age. If the child is an infant, or if the child is a teenager, there should always be clear expectations with an accountability structure.

The only way to achieve this type of training is with time. Time with the child needs to be first and foremost. How will your child know what your expectations are? Simple; you spend time talking with them and modeling that type of behavior. One of the biggest issues with bartering that I see in our current society is that when you are bartering or begging your child to behave, you are putting the two of you on an equal level. You are saying to your child that you are my equal, and therefore I have something to offer to you if you are able to behave.

Please don't misunderstand that statement. I believe that reward systems are valuable. What I'm referring to is when you consider that you and your child are equal in all things and become "friends," and therefore the bartering is based on that. There should always be a healthy fear and respect for a parental figure.

Again, as I have aged, I still remember the many times that my parents "loved on me" as a very young child. I often think about certain things that I hear children say to their parents today, that if I had even thought of those things I would have been held accountable for them. I really thought that my parents could go into my mind and hear every single thing I was thinking. That's how fearful I was of becoming a child that was going to go in the wrong direction.

The other area that I referenced above was time-out. Many parents use this system thinking that it serves a dual purpose. They think it serves the purpose of allowing the child time to reflect on their behavior and think about what they have done and gives them space. Many parents I've talked to also say it serves a dual purpose for them because it gives them time to cool off and reflect and think about what has happened. There are positives and negatives with this system. I truly believe that a time-out system should only be used when you are asking a child to go consult God in prayer. If there is a time when your child has been disobedient and has not followed the careful instruction and training that you have provided, there may need to be a "time-out period" for them to go and sit at the feet of Jesus and understand what it is that their heavenly Father is asking them to do in the context of what you've just said.

To give a time-out because you do not want to correct the child via spanking is an inappropriate use of the time-out system. However, with that being said, if the time-out period is being used for you to calm yourself down in order to not harm your child, then that is absolutely appropriate. That may be a harsh reality for some to read, but there are parents that do need to take a cool-down period to aid in the prevention of enacting discipline inappropriately.

We always want to make sure our children are safe in the context of discipline, which is why I think for our society this has become such a hot-button topic. Discipline resonates in the mind of society as abuse. They see the child as being one that is being hit upon by a person bigger and more forceful, and that we should be able to figure out ways to "talk it out." There are times when talking is all that's necessary; however, there are times that spanking is also necessary.

The key to discipline is, knowing your child. Having five children, each child is completely different as to how we discipline them. Now, remember, I indicated that discipline means to teach and to correct. In the school system, we know that there is something called "differentiated learning," where you use a certain teaching method that addresses varying needs in the classroom. The same holds true within your household, you need to use differentiated discipline. Every child may not respond to you telling them to do something; one child may respond to spanking, another child may respond to just the mention of a spanking, where another child may respond to taking items away. There is a huge laundry basket of items that you can use at your disposal for discipline.

When God tells us to not spare the rod and to promptly discipline, it is not always in the form of something that is physical. I will give you an example. One of my children needs spanking. He is one of our children that has a very strong spirit and I praise God every moment for that. But if we were to talk to our youngest son Avery and ask him what the issues were that happened at school, why he did certain things, he would articulate exactly what we needed to hear. He would have a repentant heart, but then the behavior would occur again and again. When we enacted spanking with him as a consequence for certain things he realized quickly, I do not like that, and his behavior changed very rapidly.

Same scenario, different child. One of our twins, our daughter Alyssa, has only been spanked, maybe twice in her life, and she's 13.

The reason is not because she performs and does things perfectly in our home, but because we use a different type of discipline when it is necessary. Alyssa responds to expectations that you have which are not being met as a burden upon her heart. If she knows what your expectation is and you have said to her, "Alyssa, I am disappointed with your actions," that crushes her. It doesn't crush her to the point where it breaks her spirit—and I'm using "crush" loosely—but it crushes her in a way that corrects the behavior.

The point I hope that you are seeing is that every child is different and every child responds to your teaching and correction in a different way. I want to impress upon you, prior to going into Alphabet Soup, that you should never discipline your child when you yourself are in a space of anger or distress. You should always approach discipline in a loving way with your child. When you are teaching and correcting via discipline your child should understand that this hurts you more than it may hurt them. They need to understand that because you love them, you are disciplining them; because you love them, you want the best for them; because you love them, you are enacting Godly principles within their life.

If a parent comes from a place of anger or distress or despair, the child can misinterpret that discipline as something that is against them as a person and may cause damage that you can't repair. However, if you enact discipline appropriately, as your child gets older they will understand the reasons why you did what you did and come back one day and thank you.

A B C
ALPHABET SOUP

1. Learn how to differentiate discipline. Sit down one day with your child and talk to them about the whole concept of discipline. Begin your time with prayer. Pray and ask God to enter your heart and your child's heart to be on one accord when it comes to teaching and discipline. Outline the expectations that you have in every area of your child's life. Outline for your child the expectations for school, for play, for relationships, for home, for church, for outside activities, etc.

2. Once your child understands what your expectations are, then you can have a dialogue about what happens when those expectations are not met. It's okay to have your child be a part of the correction process. If they know that not watching their favorite television show on a Friday evening would be a worse disciplinary action than a spanking, then talk to your child about how we will enact that as part of our discipline plan.

3. If there is more than one child, I cannot stress enough that you ensure that there is private time as you are talking to each of them about the discipline. There should be an overall expectation for all children within the home. I've talked a lot about differentiated discipline; however, you have to ensure that the rules are fair across the board and the expectations are consistent across all children. You don't want to have a situation where you expect one child to do one thing and another child to do something different.

4. At the end of your time meeting with each child, I would recommend a family meeting. During this family meeting, you sit and talk about the expectations of your household; what has God called your home to do and how can you manifest that with

your behavior. Even if your child is very young, you can still have this conversation and ask: How can you represent Christ in kindergarten? What can you do that would line up with what mommy and daddy teach you at home? The conversation and the tone will take a different turn if there are teenagers, because they will then begin to understand that anything that they do not only impacts their walk for Christ, but it also impacts your family name.

Chapter E

EXCELLENCE

1 CORINTHIANS 10:31—*So whether you eat or drink, or whatever you do, do everything for the glory of God.*

o you as a parent expect mediocrity or excellence out of your children? I have started to see an unfortunate trend in society where mediocrity is the norm of what we hope to achieve. Excellence, when achieved, is sometimes looked at as being braggadocios or being something that does not fit with the general population.

I affectionately recall a story that was told to me by Dr. Yvonne Callaway. She explained to me that when she was very young, her mother had a profound impact on the course of her education by demanding excellence. Dr. Calloway received a very high grade on an assignment in school one day. When she arrived home and explained to her mother that she received this high grade, her mother looked at the work and immediately was appalled. The work was not excellent, but rather, it was subpar. She took her daughter back to the school and spoke with the teacher and demanded that the teacher give her a failing grade for the work that she turned in because it was not work that exudes excellence. From that point forward in the story I could only imagine the profound impact that would have had on her to always achieve excellence, thus making her Dr. Yvonne Callaway.

As I stated earlier, it appears that the idea of not being excellent is acceptable. When we talk about striving to be better, sometimes our society thinks that we are talking about striving to be above someone, or to lord over their heads that we are better than them, where in fact there can be a distinction in taking pride for being good at doing something.

I recently recall someone asking one of my children to sign up for a sports league that did not take score. I was quite intrigued by how they would play games but not keep score, and the person who was over this endeavor indicated that society places too much emphasis on who wins and who loses, therefore we're just going to play a fun game where no one wins and no one loses, everyone can play fairly.

That was quite appalling to hear, because we should always strive to be best in everything that we do. God's Word tells us, in all that we do, we are to do it for His glory. Yes, there is a competitive edge as I say that, and I recognize that, but in no way do I put down another person as I am striving to be the best that I can be.

During a school function for our children a parent approached me and said that my son Avery is such an athletically gifted child that we need to teach him that it's okay to let others beat him, and we should strive as parents to make him understand that everyone is a winner and that everyone can beat him. I wholeheartedly agree that everyone can win at something. Everyone can be winner. As long as they are putting forth their best effort in everything, then they truly are a winner. I also agree that at times it can be a wonderful thing to humble our children to understand to share in that winning.

However, we cannot take what is striving for excellence in a child and tell them to put a cap on it because we fear that another child may not be able to achieve the same type of results. What is interesting in that parent's statement is there are certain things that their child excels in that my child may not excel in. God has created each person and each child differently. It is okay for children to desire to win and then work hard to win. This also establishes a wonderful work ethic in our children early on. We should be very aware that God would have us all strive for excellence in every area.

Since bullying is much more prevalent, I think some of these messages are getting mixed in. We are afraid that children are being picked on and children are being bullied because they are not allowed to be who they are. Sometimes who they are is not a person that fits into the mold of the norm. If you can have more of a homogenous society, where everyone looks the same, everyone acts the same, everyone does the same and everyone is accepting of everything, then most clinicians believe that would decrease bullying.

You may guess that I disagree with society and I disagree with trying to make a more homogenous society. There are so many examples in God's Word where He tells us that He has created us as different people. Yes, we have been created in His image, but He's given each of us individuality and He wants us to strive to be our best. He doesn't want us to be subpar in anything. There can be times where we believe we have an entitlement, that because of who we are we expect certain things to come to us. It could be in the form of school, for your children, it could be in the form of work for you as a parent, but either way, the only thing that we can say about entitlement is that unless God has given it to us, it is not ours to have.

Another point is how we define excellence. Do we see only the things that are important to us worth striving for, or do we know the hearts of our children well enough to be able to ask them the question about the things that they want to strive for excellence in? Excellence could be in cleaning the kitchen. Excellence could be in doing their homework. Excellence could be in folding the laundry. Excellence could mean being the best on the soccer team or the basketball team. Excellence could be baking. Excellence could be any number of things that are important to your child.

What type of things have you taken the opportunity to ask your child and cultivate excellence in your child? If your child has a love for crochet and knitting, like my Alyssa does, then help her find ways to strive for excellence in that area. I can't crochet, and I can't knit, but what I can do is support her and be her biggest cheerleader. In everything that your child does as they strive for this idea of excellence, you should be their biggest cheerleader, even when they fail. There have been times when my children have given me certain things that I may not think are excellent in my mind, but because they have put forth their best work and they've put forth the best energy and it is excellent in God's eyes, then it's excellent in my eyes.

A B C
ALPHABET SOUP

1. Sit down with your child, or children, and find out things that they want to achieve excellence within. Is it a craft? Is it a hobby? Is it a subject in school? Take them to God's Word and find scripture passages that would help to edify them as they are walking on this journey of seeking excellence. Ask them why it's important for them to achieve excellence, and then begin the process of mapping out what that looks like.

2. This is an area that may mean sacrifice for you. It may mean that you give up your monthly shopping trip to engage them

in their area of excellence. Is it a ballet recital that they're striving for? Is it a soccer tournament that they're striving for? What is it that your child wants, desires, needs? Try as a parent to have a sacrificial love for your child to help them achieve that excellence.

Chapter F

FATHERS

PROVERBS 4:1—*Hear, my children, the instruction of a father, and give attention to know understanding.*

ecently I came across some alarming statistics regarding fathers not being in the home:

- The U.S. Department of Census states that 43 percent of children in the United States live without their father.
- 90 percent of homeless and runaway children are from fatherless homes.
- 80 percent of rapists motivated with displaced anger come from fatherless homes.
- 71 percent of pregnant teenagers come from fatherless homes.
- 63 percent of youth suicides are from fatherless homes.
- 85 percent of children who exhibit behavioral disorders come from fatherless homes.[1]

Whether or not you agree or disagree with the statistics and the source that each of the statistics may have been derived from, the fact of the matter is that fathers are of vital importance within the home. I stopped because these statistics continued to go on for pages about the number of youth, dropouts, juveniles, people in prison, staggering numbers, over 80 percent, were based on the fact there was no father in the home.

I had a discussion with a few graduate students regarding this topic and they vehemently disagreed with the statistics. Their thought was it doesn't matter if there is a father in the home, a child can still thrive. My argument with them was I don't negate the fact that there are awesome mothers who are raising children by themselves and awesome fathers that are raising children by themselves, as well as awesome grandparents that are raising children without fathers. God's design, nonetheless, was to have a father and a mother in the home. There are definitely circumstances in which a father may not be in the home based upon so many factors; however, the design is still something that God had intended.

Going back to my discussion with these graduate students, they began to ask, "Well, Dr. White, do you think that a father figure would be an adequate substitute?" My response was, if a mother reaches out to individuals within a community to be a father figure for her children, then absolutely, if the father is not present in the home for whatever reason. However, at this time I want to focus just momentarily on those fathers that are living within their homes with their children but may not be as active as they need to be.

I learned the value of how important it is for a father to teach his sons based on watching my husband raise young men within our home. There was an incident that occurred many years ago when our boys were much younger. Our oldest son Alonzo has such a quiet spirit and our youngest son Avery has a more rambunctious love for life and zest for all that he does. Oftentimes, years ago, Avery would cause Alonzo to cry because he would take something that belonged to his brother; he saw it in his hand, he would walk right over and take it from him and didn't care. On one specific occasion I remember, Alonzo came out of the room that they were playing in sobbing. My husband asked what had happened. Alonzo, while crying, exclaimed, "Avery took my toy."

My husband looked at Alonzo right in his eyes and said, "Alonzo, go back in that room and get your toy." Alonzo looked terrified, as did I in the background. My husband went on to explain, "You are older, you are bigger, if you never stand up for yourself your brother will always take your toys and take everything that belongs to you; if you want your toy, go get it."

So as Alonzo went back into the room, I turned to my husband, just in fear that he was promoting fighting amongst our children and asked for further clarification. He explained that God has him in our home in order to raise godly sons and also to partner with me in raising all of our children and help raise godly women, but specifically he wants to make an impact on these young boys that will turn out to be on fire for Christ as men. He indicated that there is a "pecking order" within a sib-ship, and right now it's out of order and Alonzo needs to establish his authority over his younger brother so that he knows who in fact the big brother is.

As my husband is explaining this to me I can hear rumbling and tumbling in the background and out comes Alonzo from the room victorious with his toy. It was a concept that was baffling as a mother. As a mother, I'm a nurturer. As soon as I saw my son come out of the room the first time I wanted to run to him as he was crying and ask what was wrong and then try to fix it for him. But praise God that my husband quickly intervened and was able to help him grow into who God would call him to be.

I laugh as I recall this story because many weeks after the same exact issue happened, Alonzo was in the playing area with his younger brother and again he comes out of the room crying because once again Avery took his toy. On that particular day my husband was not home, so I immediately thought, what do I do? So I looked at Alonzo, and while holding back tears said, "Go back and get your toy." It was such an awesome moment for me as a mother to be able to take my husband's teachings and implement them. My son went back in the room and once again victoriously came out with his toy.

Many years later my 13-year-old Alonzo towers over his nine-year-old brother, but they have an affectionate love for one another because the sib-ship order has been established. Without a shadow of a doubt Alonzo is the big brother, just not in stature, but in every act and word and deed. It was an amazing transformation to see this young man grow into being confident knowing that he was the big brother; again, a lesson that a mother possibly could have taught her child, but in my own frailty and inadequacies, I would not have been able to do.

The same holds true when it comes time to talk to my three girls about issues that are happening in their life. My husband may have his perspective on what he would do, but God has given me something to give to each one of those girls that will make an impact as a godly woman in the kingdom.

Don't misunderstand, when I say that fathers have an important value, that I mean the only place they have that value is to raise sons. Fathers set the tone for the home. If we look in the book of Ephesians, we understand that there is an order, that God commands husbands to be held accountable underneath God for how his home is structured. Wives, we are to submit. That is not a word that should cause us to cringe, but it should be a word that causes us to celebrate. Are we going to willingly align ourselves underneath our husband's authority in order for our home to flourish the way God has intended? We have two choices. We can either challenge the system or we can bend underneath his authority and begin the process of learning how to listen amongst our own flesh. It's an amazing transformation when we understand that God holds the father accountable.

I receive a lot of resistance when I speak about this topic because there are so many women that believe that they can do a better job than a man at raising a son; that they understand the type of man that they want their sons to be and they can do a better job. I disagree. I disagree because God has a purpose for our sons and unless we can humble ourselves to understand that we may need assistance to see certain nuances in our sons that we may not see if we aren't submissive to God, we'll miss the entire mark.

Society wants us to believe that fathers are not important. Think about your three favorite television shows right now. Think about each of them, and think about the role that fathers have within the context of the television show. For me, as I'm writing this book, I can vividly think of several television shows where the husband is made to look like a fool; he is not the decision maker in the home, he is not the one who has sage wisdom, but it's either the wife or the children; the husband is supposed to just crawl into the corner with his remote control in his man cave. Please do not succumb to what the world's view is of fatherhood. Fathers are important.

I would be remiss if I did not talk about the importance that fathers play in the lives of their daughters. It is amazing to watch my three daughters just take every moment that they spend with their father and cherish it. I love watching their interaction. When a father has a close relationship with a daughter their self-esteem rises and any young boy that comes after their heart, they should compare to their father. And so if the father is living for Christ and is living in a way that is godly submission, any boy, any man, that is after that daughter's heart is going to have to measure up to dad. If dad sets the bar high, the daughter will set the bar high. Fathers, you are so important in the role that you play with your princess.

A B C
ALPHABET SOUP

1. If there's not a father that is living within the home, then find someone within your local church, YMCA or school system that would spend time mentoring your young sons, your teenaged sons. It would be imperative for their growth to see the mindset of a man coming alongside to assist in that process.

2. Set up playdates with other fathers and sons. In order to raise these godly men there needs to be a structure of accountability that they understand very, very young. What I mean by accountability is if we're going out with the same dad and sons and we're going to a Bible study, we're going to have fun together, then we will be able to pray in areas that maybe mom and sister can't because we are now in fellowship and accountability with this small group of people.

3. You should also have dedicated time with your son inside and outside the home. Be a father that is at school. Be a father that will take the time to pour into, not just your sons and daughters, but other sons and daughters.

Chapter G

GRATEFULNESS

1 THESSALONIANS 5:18—*In everything give thanks; for this is the will of God in Christ Jesus for you.*

A lot can be told about a person and their upbringing by how grateful they are. Interestingly enough, our attitude about being grateful is immediately passed down from generation to generation. I'm not speaking of some inherent gene that is within us that's passed down, but an attitude and lifestyle that is lived out in front of children on a daily basis.

My family teases me incessantly when we go to restaurants. When we go to a restaurant I want the waiter or the waitress to feel so special, that I thank them continuously throughout our meal for doing such a good job. If they've gone above and beyond I will typically call the manager over and express my gratitude towards them. My family will tease me and will mock sometimes my voice with one another and role-play waiter and mommy. We all find it quite funny. However, on a more serious note, what that models for my children is that I appreciate immensely a job that someone does.

God has blessed us in so many ways that my children have not had to endure some of the hardships that we had to endure as children, mainly in the financial realm, always praising God for allowing us to have jobs that will afford us little things, such as purchasing clothing that the children may like, purchasing of electronic equipment that they desire. I am grateful that God has seen fit to trust us with some of these earthly possessions. But because of that we express to our kids where it all comes from; it comes from above. It doesn't come from the hard work that we put in, it doesn't come from anything that we wished; it comes truly from God extending His grace and mercy into the life of a sinner.

A heart that is grateful to God is a heart that can be used for God. We express this and show this to our children on a repetitive basis. I am grateful and thank God for every moment of every day. I am grateful for every crumb that I eat, every accident that I go by on the highway, that He provided safety for my family. My children hear me express this verbally, that there is not one thing that I take for granted. My husband and I will often express bad things within the news to our children as a way for them to understand that only by the grace of God that we are where we are. We begin to pray for those who have been afflicted by tragedy. We pray for those who have had afflictions in any area of their life. And also, we thank Him, that He's allowed us to have a voice to be able to thank Him.

We take for granted so many different things that I truly believe that if we had the ability to go into multiple homes across the world and see all the differences of how we have been blessed, we would then be more grateful. I never take for granted being able to hear the birds chirping. I never take for granted being able to see a sunset.

When our oldest son Alonzo was born, he had a lot of difficulties after birth. His bilirubin level went up to 45. Bilirubin is a brownish yellow substance found in bile. It is produced when the liver breaks down old red blood cells. Bilirubin is then removed from the body through the stool and gives the stool its normal color. When bilirubin levels are high, the skin and whites of the eyes may appear yellow or jaundiced. Jaundice happens when the bilirubin builds up faster than a newborn's liver can break it down and pass it from the body.

In Alonzo's case, he and I had blood incompatibility. My blood type was different than his and I produced antibodies that were destroying his red blood cells. This caused his bilirubin level to rise. We were told that a normal bilirubin was around 1 or 2. We were advised that a bilirubin over 20 was extremely dangerous and most often resulted in cerebral palsy. Imagine our horror and shock when we were told our newborn son's bilirubin level was 45. This was the highest bilirubin that the University of Michigan Hospital system had ever seen. Alonzo is still, 13 years later, being remembered as the little boy that they never thought would make it. Upon having him checked back into the ER only five days after giving birth, he was in intensive care fighting for his life. I vividly remember that night, the doctor said because his bilirubin level was so high he was not going to make it through the night. We immediately began to call everyone that we knew to begin praying for our little newborn son. We had to bring his twin sister to the hospital to also be tested, and had our first moment of gratitude that our Lord was so gracious and spared her this affliction. We had no idea what He was going to do with Alonzo.

At that time Alonzo required several full body blood transfusions to allow him to live. The next hurdle after having these blood transfusions was, that because the bilirubin was so high, they said that he would be deaf and that he would have significant cognitive damage as well, most likely cerebral palsy. We were grateful. We were grateful that God spared his life and that He would allow us to raise a beautiful little boy. He was our first son and we named him after my husband's grandfather, Alonzo Parham. We were overjoyed that even though he would not be able to hear and would have cognitive limitations, that we would raise him in such a way that would bring honor and glory to God.

Little did we know that God was listening and watching our grateful hearts and would turn our lives all around. Alonzo had minimal hearing after leaving the hospital, but nonetheless, my husband was determined that he was going to play every sport possible. That even if he had to sign the plays on the side of the football, basketball, soccer, baseball field, that is what he was going to do, because we had a heart of gratitude that He gave us a son. He gave us another child. We had a beautiful five-year-old little girl, and we had a beautiful newborn little girl, but now He's given us yet another child, that being a boy, who would carry on the family name.

As we employed several therapists into our home over a year's period of time, we tried to adjust to life with a child that was severely hearing impaired. Not much sound would actually get through until one day I remember the phone rang and Alonzo immediately turned to the phone's ringing. I rejoiced, called my husband and shouted, "Alonzo can hear, Alonzo can hear." One of my closest friends, Felecia Frederick, was there in my home at that time and rejoiced with me that he actually could hear. As we went back to University of Michigan Hospital, they couldn't explain why he had regained hearing. It was as if a light switch had been turned on in his ears and he gained full hearing. Isn't God amazing? As we continued to proclaim the goodness of God, and explain to the hospital staff that it could only be God, they were truly, still not believing.

I believe what happened next was God's design, because if Alonzo had remained with normal hearing we wouldn't have had the opportunity to go back and live out our gratefulness and our lifestyle in front of the University of Michigan Hospital staff. Three and a half years later Alonzo's hearing started to fail again. At that time, it was recommended that he wear bilateral hearing aids. We obtained the hearing aids and a beautiful personality began to blossom in this little four-year-old boy. He went from being a boy that appeared to be shy and quiet to a boy that could not stop talking. And at the age of 13, he is still the same picture of a little boy that cannot stop talking. It is the most glorious thing.

What God has allowed to happen is that even though Alonzo remains hearing impaired, we are connected to the University of Michigan health care system. On a regular basis we live out our faith and our gratitude to God for what He has done in our lives in front of the hospital staff. It is an amazing thing.

Do you have a story of gratitude? Do you have something that has happened within your family that you can look back and see God's hand and you're just grateful that He has taken you through? I ask that because it was at that moment that God took us through a difficult period of time that I understood what it meant to be grateful for just opening my eyes and being able to hear. When my son couldn't hear, I was able to. I understood in the moment, when I was able to reach for something with my hands, that there were people that did not have hands. I understood, as I could walk places, that there were people that were amputees that could not. I have had a heart that has been directed at God for being grateful for everything that He does.

One of the many benefits of having a grateful heart is that it changed my prayer life. I wanted to truly understand what it meant to pray without ceasing according to what God's Word says. If I am grateful that He woke me, then I need to pray and thank Him in thanksgiving for doing so. If I'm grateful for the food that I am eating, I want to pray and ask Him what would glorify Him for me to put into my body. If I'm grateful for walking on two legs, I want to pray and ask Him how do I maintain where I am with these legs and where does He want my legs to go.

It truly altered the way that I began to think as a mother about the lives of my children. I was grateful for being given five awesome kids that are all saved, baptized and serving Him in the capacity of our church, but my prayer life changed with that gratitude. I wanted to know how He would want me to utilize each gift that was given to each child, and how I would as a mother help them live up to their fullest potential as a Christian. It was an exciting time to have a new lease on a new prayer life that has been rooted in gratitude.

A B C
ALPHABET SOUP

1. Make a list of all the things that God has done for you in your adult life. Make a list of all the things that He has done for you since you've been saved. Make this list so personal that you can't help but scream, "Thank you Jesus" as you're writing.

2. Once you make this list, put it somewhere that's visible. We have a tendency—and I'm saying "we" because I am included— that when we hit a trial, instead of doing what James 1:2 says, to count it all joy when we fall into various trials, we will moan, we will groan, we will sulk, and we will sometimes forget what God has done. So I would recommend, for you and for your children, that you make this list visible. Have your child do the exact same list, and maybe you put your lists together.

3. Create a family gratitude board, where everyone puts the things that God has done, the prayers that God has answered. And so as you hit those adversities, those difficult times in life, you can go right to your gratitude board and scream, "Thank you Jesus."

4. Teach your child how to say, "Thank you" at the same time they learn "mommy" and "daddy." Saying the words "Thank you" does not require effort, it requires repetition.

Chapter H

HOME

PSALM 128:1–4—*How blessed is everyone who fears the LORD, who walks in His ways. When you shall eat of the fruit of your hands, you will be happy, and it will be well with you. Your wife shall be like a fruitful vine within your home, your children like olive plants around your table. Behold, for thus shall the man be blessed who fears the LORD.*

Over the years I have listened to Pastor Tony Evans. There have been so many impactful sermons that I have listened to, but none more impactful than the day that I listened to a sermon based solely on those four verses above. Dr. Tony Evans indicated that the husband is responsible for setting the tone of the home, and therefore is the first focal point of Psalm 128. When the husband is centered by God and fears God and walks with God, there is an automatic response that will come from the wife, according to Dr. Evans.[1]

The image that God gives in His Word is that of a grapevine. A grapevine always clings. The atmosphere in a home is that a woman should be able to wrap her branches around her husband. Dr. Evans goes on to state that a wife who hangs on to her husband and wraps around him totally is doing what God wants, because God wants wives to be clinging vines. I love the next picture that Dr. Evans gives. He indicates that vines not only cling, but they climb. When the man is in right fellowship with God, the wife wants to cling, and then she grows. She develops strengths, abilities and skills. She becomes a better woman than she was before.

Lastly, Dr. Evans mentions that a grapevine also clusters and provides grapes for wine. If a husband lets his wife cling and climb, she'll cluster and make him drunk with her love. Isn't that a beautiful word picture that Dr. Evans gives us about God's Word? Imagine children living in that type of environment. This would be an environment where the father, as the head of the household, is in right fellowship with God. As this occurs, his wife automatically clings to the husband, climbs into the purpose for which God has called her, and then clusters and provides what God has called her to give her family.

I think about how this whole process in Psalm 128 can be accomplished, and I can't think of a better place than around the family dinner table. It is amazing that there is so much that can take place at the family dinner table. I was happily pleased, as I attended an event where Dr. Evans spoke in 2015, that he also referenced the family table as an important growth point for their family. I was pleased because this has been something that my husband and I have been very intentional about since our first daughter was born 18 years ago. And as we've introduced other children into our home, five children later our dinner table has many nicks and cuts and bruises and dents, but is still a solid and beautiful place where we gather.

What has happened to that concept of a dinner table in society? It appears that because of the modern family's busy lifestyle, we have taken the dinner table on the road. Families have soccer, basketball, baseball, track, dance, gymnastics—fill in the blank. Families have every imaginable activity after school that keeps their children very busy, many times three and four days a week. For families that have multiple children, you may say that sounds like my life, we are carpooling or we're taking kids and we eat on the run.

We also see in our generation this concept of when we are at home and when we are at the dinner table, we're distracted. We are connected to our electronic devices or we're connected to the television, or we may even be connected to what's going on outside of our home at our neighbor's home. There are so many distractions, that we push away this whole concept of coming together at the dinner table. Eighteen years ago we purposed to be different and we purposed to be a family that would be an impact family in the kingdom of God. I'm happy to say that the rules that we have set forth for our dinner table have been valuable for our children and other children.

Rule number one for us is there are no electronics allowed at the table and no television allowed during that time. I have to be honest and say that I have broken this rule several times attempting to return a "quick" text message or view an email.

Rule number two is, one person talks at a time. We can't have everyone trying to chime in about their day. We're respectful of each other and we take turns.

Rule number three is, everyone talks. We ensure that even our youngest child has a voice, and our oldest child doesn't get lost. So we balance that by everyone taking a turn and talking about their day. As a parent, it is at this time that I am listening, not only with my ears, but I'm listening with my eyes. As a psychologist, I have been trained to look at the total body and to see how the body moves and how the body interacts with the speech, because there is so much that can be said about body language and parts of speech. So as I sit there I'm watching how they interact. I'm listening to what they're saying and how they're saying it.

My husband and I use this time at the dinner table as an opportunity in several ways:

First, it's an opportunity to talk about God. In every instance that occurs with our children we use it as a moment to, either glorify God, give honor to God, or talk about what God was trying to teach them through an adversity or through a success.

Secondly, it gives us an opportunity to teach them how to act properly when they leave the home. As I started the book, if you recall in the introduction, I mentioned the compliments that we will get when we go out to eat. That didn't just happen overnight. It has been from our dinner table. It has been a teaching and a constant correction at the dinner table. We'll teach our children to have both feet on the floor. We'll teach our children to sit straight in the chair. We'll teach them what utensils to use and when, and how to properly look someone in the eye when you're speaking with them.

Third, we recognize that the dinner table also serves as a way to help them with any social awkwardness that they may have. If they are taking cues from their siblings and waiting until it's time to speak, if they're adding value to what their siblings are saying or to what we as parents are saying, then we are helping further them along in the different stages where it may be socially awkward in middle school to have those type of relationships. We're helping them understand how to respect authority as they're talking about things that may have happened that they didn't like with their teachers or with their coaches. The family dinner table has such a wonderful value that I could write a book just about the dinner table.

So you're probably wondering to yourself, if my family is one of those families that does have the dinner table on the road, is all hope lost; absolutely not. You still need to find time that you can carve out, even if you make the dinner table 25 minutes in a moving van, where the radio goes off, where the electronics are put away, and as you are eating you tell them, this is our dinner table time and this is what we're going to do during our dinner table time: We're not going to negate the fact that we need it, we're going to make sure that we have it, and for the next 25 minutes on the way to your game we're going to have our dinner table time. The main objective is to make the dinner table time a consistent part of everyday life, whether it's at home or on the road.

A B C
ALPHABET SOUP

1. Pick a day that you will start a new dinner table tradition in your family. From that, purpose in your heart that this is something that you want to make a permanent part of your lives. The reason that I ask you to purpose in your heart, because the next step that's most crucial, is that you're going to pray that God will remove all distractions; you will pray that God provides a smooth path to being able to achieve those things that He has called you and your family to accomplish within that dinner table time.

2. Involve your children. Ask them to pick the day that you start. Make a calendar. If you know that during the week you're going to be extremely busy, then maybe you start off your week with sitting down with each other at the table for family dinner time, or breakfast time, or lunch time. After that, plan on your calendar if it will be at a soccer game, basketball game. Wherever

it may be, carve out those 15 to 20 minutes to connect with one another minus the outside distractions.

The benefit that you will see will not only be for your own children. We have had children outside of our family who are friends of our children visit and they will just fall in and be a part of the dinner table time. Some of them have said they've never seen anything like a family dinner table. Therefore, you can be a conduit for change within your own neighborhood.

Chapter I

INVOLVED

DEUTERONOMY 6:6–7—*And these words which I command you today shall be on your heart. You shall teach them diligently to your children, and shall talk of them when you sit in your house, when you walk by the way, when you lie down, and when you rise up.*

What is your definition of being involved in your child's life? As I look at the world that we live in, I think we as parents sometimes confuse getting a child involved versus being involved. Let me clarify my statement. We tend to think that we are "good parents" or exhibiting good parenting when our child is involved in an array of activities. We will have them involved in sports, in dance, in culinary arts; we will even have them involved in various academic extracurricular activities, such as a reading club, a chess club, a science club, or an engineering camp.

Don't misunderstand, these are good things to have your child be a part of; however, the danger becomes when that takes the place of us being involved with them. Are you involved with your child to the point where you have taken an active role in each of these areas? For example, have you enrolled your son in Boy Scouts and you became the den leader, or one of the den workers, or have you decided that you would rather drop them off on Saturday or Sunday for the meeting and come back and pick them up? When there is a field trip at your child's school, have you decided that you will be the mother that will volunteer, or the father that will be a chaperone and drive?

I'm affectionately smiling as I reminisce most recently when our second-grader, Autumn, had a field trip to the Ringling Brothers Circus in Auburn Hills. Autumn was excited bringing home the permission slip and turned to her dad and asked her dad to take the day off and go with her. What this would mean is that he would have to miss the entire day, as the field trip required a full day's involvement. My husband, without hesitation said yes, and ended up being the chaperone for four children on that day. There were three giggly little girls and one shy little boy. Part way through the field trip he texted to let me know that all was going well and that it was a literal mom-fest because there were rarely any dads that decided to take a whole day off and be at the field trip. Nonetheless, he was quite happy to make his little princess smile.

We have purposed in our family to be involved in every aspect possible of our children's lives, and what that means for us is that we rearrange our work schedules in order to accommodate almost every field trip that our children are involved in. If there are trips that require a longer commitment, then we will do our best to rearrange our schedules to accommodate. Of course there have always been some extenuating circumstances that may not allow for our general rule, but part of our heart calling to want to go on these trips is that we want our children to know that the time that we have with them is precious and that we are constantly pouring into them things that God has given us on a regular basis, and for us to adequately do that we always want to be surrounded by the people they're surrounded by as they're growing and then making impacts in whatever environment that we can with them.

If you're reading this book and scratching your head trying to determine which parent you are, ask your child if they feel that you are involved with them. Do you partner with them when it comes to sports? Do you partner with them when it comes to their academic club? Is it, "Mom and dad, we are going to this game today," or "Mom and dad, I am going to this game today." You can fill in the blank with whatever endeavor your child is a part of. It is a very easy switch once you're cognizant of the fact that you need to be involved with your child.

Clinically speaking, many of the children that have come into my office over the years have complained that their parents are not close to them based on involvement. As I probe a little further I come to find out that many of the parents that have put their children in therapy over the years have parented from afar. The makeup of the family can vary: two-parent homes where they both work, single-parent homes, multiple children that are involved in multiple activities. The parent feels that it's almost impossible to be involved in the child's life, therefore when issues arise that affect their self-esteem, that affect their levels of anxiety and stress and the child begins to suffer, the parent begins to wonder what went wrong. As we peel back the layers of the onion during the therapy session it becomes very evident that the child wants to have that parent close and an involved part of their life.

In order to understand the environment that your child dwells within you need to be a part of every aspect of the environment. If 20 percent of their environment is absorbed within an academic after-school experience, then you need to be involved in that endeavor. In bigger families with multiple children and multiple activities, choose those areas which are primary for your children and be involved in them.

Another thought for families is that we may need to limit the number of activities our children are in, in order to stay a part of those activities. Our children do not need to have activities from sun up to sun down to stimulate them and to promote growth. In our big family of five children, every child is allowed to be involved in one major activity at a time. By virtue of us being a musical family, piano lessons, piano playing, or other musical endeavors, are always a wonderful adjunct to whatever they do, therefore it is never counted as an activity, per se. Our children understand that they can be involved in a crochet ministry, play on the school basketball team, be a part of a soccer league or take gymnastics, and still participate in musical desires.

I must comment on involvement within the school. Involvement within the context of your children's education is vitally important. It appears that many teachers will complain that parents leave teaching solely to the teacher, when in fact it needs to be a partnership between home and school. The involvement that you have within your children's education will bring such a wonderful dividend at the end. Get to know your child's teacher. Go into the classroom often. Not only as a volunteer for fun activities, but go in as a reader; go in and find out the pulse of the classroom. Therefore, when your child begins to have difficulties you then can understand how to help them navigate the difficulties because you understand the pulse of the teacher and of the classroom.

When all five of my children were in the same school, I wanted to do more. I decided to become a member of the board of directors for Washtenaw Christian Academy. I had multiple "irons in the fire" at the time that I ran for a seat on the board; therefore, it seemed odd that I would accept the call to be a part of the board of directors. As I prayed about this I felt that it was God's calling and leading to be a part of such a great group of individuals that are all serving God trying to bring about change in the kingdom.

I have, and continue to enjoy my time being on the board of directors of Washtenaw Christian Academy. Being a board member has given me a different perspective, just not on my children's education, but on the education of all children. It has taken my "involvement" to a different level that engages my children on a different level. There is an appreciation that not only does mom care about what happens within our classroom, but mom cares about what happens wherever we are in any classroom in any part of the school and mom will work hard to affect change in those areas.

I'm not recommending that every single person reading this book go and join the board of directors of their local school district. However, I hope that I've made the point that involvement doesn't have to stop with being a volunteer on field trips, but it should be much more than that.

Another area that is closely linked to this concept of involvement is commitment. Once your child gets involved in an activity there is a commitment that needs to occur that is an individual and a family commitment. This is an area of great growth for me. When our oldest daughter became involved in basketball early on in high school my husband made a comment to her. He stated that if she signs up for this sport, no matter what, she's going to stick with this sport even if she doesn't like it. He told her that she committed to a team, she committed to be a part of something that is bigger than her, and once she becomes part of the team it's no longer about Alexia.

That was a hard lesson for me because there were certain times when she didn't want to go to practice or she didn't want to go to a game because we as a family had other activities. There were birthdays that would come up. There would be other engagements that I deemed, as a mother, more important to the fabric of our family than, as I would call it, a silly little basketball game. However, my husband made a point of never distinguishing between attendance at a practice or a game. He always instilled in her, and every one of our children, that a practice is just as important as a game. And he would further indicate that if you're going to skip a practice, then I would recommend to your coach that you not play in the game.

This concept of commitment, again, was a very hard one for me as a mother to digest, but I praise God for the loving guiding hands of my husband as their father to push them to be committed to things. As my daughter went through high school and became involved in other activities, that whole commitment concept became part of the fabric of her personality. She became a person that would stick with everything and never quit. It then transcended into her academics, to the point where she graduated as valedictorian of her high school class. This concept of commitment continues as she's in college, where she is completely 100 percent committed to anything that she starts; whether it's an intramural activity or a dance guild or an academic pursuit, she is completely committed.

As my sons are coming along with sports, it's the same idea and the same concept. I have now accepted that on Mother's Day there will always be a soccer game and I will have to, in part share in the joy of being a soccer mom while being celebrated by my son. It has been a bittersweet growth process because selfishly, my last Mother's Day, I wanted the day to be spent with all of my children all day doing what mommy desired. But the joy that my son had when I was able to spend half the day with him, and then send him off and tell him to win the game for mommy on Mother's Day, brought me such an internal joy. And by the way, he did win for mommy and scored two goals.

Far too many times I see parents decide that if my child doesn't like something they can just leave, they can get out, it doesn't matter because it's "just a game" or "just an activity," and we have other things that we can be doing other than allowing for this commitment to an activity. I understand completely because I thought that. I failed to recognize how

God would use commitment to a task to transform my children for His kingdom. It appears in our world that we have commitment-phobia. We're afraid to commit to anything, let alone have our children commit to something that would have vital importance for them in their growth.

A B C
ALPHABET SOUP

1. The first area to focus on is are you involved with your children or do you get your children involved. If you want to make the move to getting your children, not only involved but being involved, pick an activity that you can begin today to find a little bit more about and how you can take a more active role as a parent.

2. There may need to be a shifting in how many activities that you have your children involved in. If there are multiple children within the home, take a look at how you can scale down the activities that would still allow for intellectual, spiritual and emotional physical growth within your child, but would allow for you to have the maximum involvement within that sphere for your child.

3. If your child is involved in any activity, commit as a parent to have them stay committed. The long range and long term benefits are amazing, as I described above with our oldest daughter. Once they have committed, have them pray about who they are in Christ and what does that mean to be a committed Christian, and what testimony that will show those who are involved about being a light for Christ and an ambassador for Christ.

Chapter J

JOSHUA 24:15

<hr>

JOSHUA 24:15—*But as for me and my house, we will serve the LORD.*

You may find it odd that the title for this chapter is actually the same as the verse for the chapter. The reason that I have boldly proclaimed Joshua 24:15 as the title for Chapter J, is because it stands out as our family verse. What does your family stand for is the question. What is it that defines your family and makes you different than the other families that are around you?

As I watch the news, I see many celebrity families identified by certain things. I won't give ink to all of those messages within the context of this book, but you can imagine for yourself. It is sad to see that a family legacy can be summed up in tragedy lived out in front of millions of people.

I think specifically about one entertainer in particular, Whitney Houston. I think about the fact that her daughter has recently died this year, and I wonder what type of family life they had and what their family verse might have been. The family verse is what defines your family, what dictates the motives of your family, what dictates how you breathe as a family, how you are connected as a family. As I look at the sad exchange of information from social networks about the death of Whitney Houston and Bobby Brown's daughter, it saddens me to see that there was a pattern that the daughter followed all the way up until death.

What is it that your family holds most dear? What is it that your family holds onto that defines you in the eyes of society? I remember one summer, and you may recall this summer as well, it was the summer in the Midwest where all the lights went out. No one knew what had happened in all of the Midwest area, all the way to the east coast. All we knew was that there was a severe blackout and no one had lights or any type of power. Well, I remember at that time living in a cul-de-sac where there were only six homes. All six of us knew each other by glance and by wave. A few of us had relationships with each other as neighbors. We had been consistent in how we lived as a Christian family and knew that we were looked upon in that cul-de-sac as a Christian family. People would see us go to church every Sunday morning at the same time. People would see us dressed up in such a way that they might assume we were going to church. But on that day when the lights went out, the lights came on for me in my mind.

As the lights went out, all the neighbors quickly ran outside to see if there was something going on outside. We ended up congregating outside where it was much cooler. One of our neighbors looked at us and said, "Okay, the rapture didn't happen because your family is still here." I chuckle about this many years later. The truth of the matter is I did not have a relationship with this neighbor at all. I saw them; I knew they were my neighbor. I didn't even know their first or last name, but

I knew them as, "Hi neighbor." They knew us in the same way. What I failed to understand was that they were watching our family verse being lived out day in and day out in that area.

What an amazing testimony for a family. I'm not saying that because it's a testimony about my family, but it's a testimony about my God. We can't take any credit for what God has called us to do that gives Him back the glory. I'm so thankful and I'm so grateful that He gave us that opportunity to live that out in that neighborhood.

When your family walks into a room what images are conjured? Do people turn and walk away because you're the family that gossips all the time and they don't want to hear yet more gossip about someone in the family? Are you the family that when you walk in the door people just sigh and say, wow, here they come, they're so negative, they use profanity constantly and they're just negative and they drain me? Or are you the family, that when you walk in the door people are excited for what you are about to share, that they know that there is refuge found within your family because you are able to usher in the presence of God based on your praise and worship to Him.

Are people excited to see your family? What defines your family? Every family needs to have a family verse. Every family needs to understand that their verse should pave the walkway to their driveway. Your verse should pave the walkway to your bedrooms. I have Joshua 24:15 in probably 10 or more places within my home, whether it's stenciled on a wall, or a placard that hangs in the kitchen, or another reminder above the children's bedroom, outside the laundry room; it is something that is permanently enmeshed within our family, that by the time you're walking you're able to say Joshua 24:15.

A B C
ALPHABET SOUP

1. My challenge to you is to find something in God's Word that you can cling to that defines you as a family. What is it that you would want to strive towards as a family? What are the goals that God has placed within you to impact His kingdom for good? To live within this house you need to be on board, knowing who your personal Lord and Savior is. That doesn't mean that you're forced into a relationship, but you have been in an environment that will allow that willing submission, voluntary submission, as God paints the picture of submission in His Word, a voluntary submission underneath God's authority to be able to be impactful for His kingdom.

2. Once you find your family verse, put it everywhere. Say it all the time. Share it with your children. Make a crossword puzzle, make a coloring book, make it practical for them, that they will be able to hide His Word in their heart.

Chapter **K**

KINDNESS

GALATIANS 5:22—*But the fruit of the spirit is love, joy, peace, longsuffering, kindness, goodness, faithfulness, gentleness, self-control, against such there is no law.*

Sometimes I think I live in too simplistic of a world. I want people to be kind in all circumstances, but I realize that that's not the reality. With each of my five children, God has fashioned their hearts to be sensitive in ways that their friends' words or actions can be like daggers to their heart. I recall often each child saying at one time or another that a child was mean to them or hurt their feelings. Now, knowing my mama bear personality, in each of those cases I have gone to the school and investigated and spoken with not only the teacher, but possibly the parent and the child, to find out if what my child had said was true. Fortunately, or unfortunately, I was able to verify that in most cases what my child had stated was true.

Knowing that there were unkind words spoken sometimes seems like no big deal in the society that we live in. After all, it is those unkind words that get the loudest laughter on sitcoms; the more insulting that we can be, the more things that we can say to berate people and to degrade them, the louder the laugh track will be in the background of the sitcom.

This is one of the reasons that we—as I will talk about in Chapter M, Media—have curtailed so much of the television that our children are even allowed to watch on a regular basis. We do not want those types of unkind images to infiltrate our home. Have you thought about the type of home that your child is dwelling within? Is it a home that allows for kindness, or is it a home that allows for degrading and berating for the sake of "playing the dozens"?

We, as parents, have a responsibility to exercise the fruit of the spirit. And what I mean by "exercise" the fruit of the spirit, is that we are putting these things on, on a daily basis. It is more than just cloaking our bodies with them, but as we do with exercise, we are utilizing them. We're utilizing them in a repetitive motion. We're making sure that we are bathed daily with self-control, with gentleness, with loving kindness. These are the qualities that Christ has. Are we teaching our children to truly be ambassadors like Christ and show kindness?

I often wonder when it comes to little boys, if we as a society have swayed them towards being unkind as a way to maintain their "manliness." I have often heard it said that being macho and being kind should not coexist. Shouldn't we be teaching our boys to find a healthy balance between the two?

I've seen many people come in for counseling, often they are unable to remember kind things that have been said to them throughout their childhood. It is typically the unkind things that they have heard from their peers, from their teachers, from their family members on a repetitive basis that have seared into their brain an image of them as a person. Then 20 years later, they are seeking counseling because their self-esteem has been trampled upon. I would love for us to understand the correlation between low self-esteem and the things that we hear that are put upon our psyche.

In my son Avery's classroom, his fourth grade teacher, Miss Elie, has created a wonderful vehicle to promote kindness amongst the students. She asks each of them to write kind words about their classmates on a piece of paper. By the time the exercise has finished each child has an entire page full of kind words that have been written about them. At first when my son brought home his filled page of kind words I didn't understand the impact until he had a bad day and pulled those words out and looked at some of the kind things that his classmates had written. They wrote about his character and about him as an individual. The look on Avery's face each time he looked upon those words is priceless. He transformed into a young boy that is holding on to the good things that people are saying as opposed to the negatives that people may spew. It was a wonderful tool to teach a nine-year-old. Each time that there has been a struggle in that fourth grade classroom, I too have turned to that paper and said look at what this young boy or girl said about you. I remind him that if they said these kind words about you, maybe they had a bad day when they uttered the negative words.

The most important part of this chapter is to understand that the only way for your children to be kind is for them to see you being kind first. Your children emulate everything that you do. It's very interesting to watch children navigate through life like their parents. If they are not able to see kindness being extended to others from their parents, how do we expect them to then extend kindness to others? I'm sad to say that I have seen many a time when adults refuse to extend kindness to a stranger, or when an adult refuses to extend kindness to a family member, a church member, a classmate, or a coworker. Many times we have to look on the inside of ourselves to determine what it is that blocks us from being kind to someone.

If we are blocked in that area of being kind to others, then it's impossible for us to be able to share that type of pathway with our children. We can't be parents that say do as I say, not as I do. If we are serious about living for Christ and raising Christ-focused children, then we have to understand that the fruit of the spirit begins with us. The kindness that you portray to others should be effortlessly done in front of your children. They should be able to see that mom or dad is able to be kind as part of who Christ called them to be. It should never be a show. It should never be something that you're waiting to get applause for, but it should come from an outpouring of gratitude because Christ has saved you.

When your children begin to see that your natural inclination is geared toward kindness, you will be amazed that when they're faced with a similar situation, that their natural inclination will be to follow mom and dad and be kind to someone. So many times I think about the parable of the Good Samaritan. This was a remarkable story about an individual who stopped and was kind to someone in need. They helped someone who was not even associated with them, someone very different from them. They were able to stop and put aside all of the history between the two populations and be kind.

It amazes me that sometimes we as individuals cannot do that. We look upon each other and we see race. We look upon each other and we see culture. We look upon each other and we see many differences that impede us from being kind, and then we pass that on to our children. We tell our children that certain people are not worthy of a smile, that certain people are not worthy of a handshake, that certain people are not worthy of—you fill in the blank. The sad part is that in many cases we support our unkind treatment of others with scripture. We may use different scripture passages to point out why there should be a division and why there always will be a division.

The easiest way to extend kindness is with a smile. I am proud of the fact that my children know how to look at a stranger in the eye and offer a smile to each person that passes by. It may be frustrating at times if the smile is not reciprocated, but nonetheless the smile is not for them, the smile is to remind my child that inside of them dwells God's love and from that it exudes kindness. They may have planted a seed in that stranger's life that that stranger needed that day. They may not be able to recall every person that walked by them and smiled, but to have a child do it, or even to have an adult do it, may burn in that person's memory head for the rest of the day. It may cause them to possibly go back and repent, or for them to go back and then pass it forward and be kind to the next person.

A B C
ALPHABET SOUP

1. Kindness starts with you. Show kindness to strangers, show kindness to your family, show kindness to your coworkers, to your church members, to your church leadership, in front of your children. Do not do it in a way like the Pharisees, that you're bragging; but do it in such a way that it is a natural part of who you are. If it is hard for kindness to be a natural part of who you are, then begin to pray that God changes your heart to be kind, that He make kindness a part of who you are.

2. Be kind to your child. I have given many examples of how you as a parent should be kind to others outside of your home, but also be kind to your child and be kind to your spouse. Exercising that type of kindness within the context of your home begins the process of transferring that out into the community and being kind to strangers.

Chapter **L**

LISTEN

JAMES 1:19—*Understand this, my dear brothers and sisters: You must all be quick to listen, slow to speak, and slow to get angry.*

I recall one day sitting in a restaurant during lunchtime by myself. I love to look around restaurants that are crowded and just people watch and see the different interactions that people have with their children and with their spouses. You can pick up so much about a family and their structure just based on body language and dynamics of voice tone and observation.

On this particular day I remember a little boy with the cutest blonde locks trying to get his mother's attention. The whole time the mother is on her cell phone. I'm not sure what she was doing on her cell phone, but the little boy only wanted his mother's attention for a moment to listen. He kept saying, "Mommy, mommy, listen to me, listen to me, listen to me," and he kept saying it over and over and over. It was the type of repetition that made me, as a mother, want to jump up and say, "I'll listen to you." It tugged at my heart so much that it made me very aware that when my own children are asking for me to give them attention that I need to listen.

We have seen that type of dyad with children so many times in our society that it's become the norm. That sometimes the expression, children are meant to be seen and not heard, is taken to the extreme. Many people truly do feel that they don't have to take the time to listen to a child. As I counsel different children and bring their parents into the session, the child will begin to say something to the parent and the parent will immediately interrupt and try to explain their side. I will caution the parent that their job is to listen. The child will then continue to explain how they felt about a certain encounter and then the parent, most often in my counseling sessions will say, "Why didn't you tell me that?" And again, most often I hear a child respond, "I did. You weren't listening." So powerful are those statements between children and parents that I can recount a number of times in sessions where I have heard this type of conversation and it resonates in my memory.

Parents sometimes will do one of two things: We will over-talk our child to avoid listening in order to be the "parental figure" that knows best and neglect to hear our child, or we may be so wrapped up in our own busyness of life that our child may be communicating to us and we do not hear.

There are several ways that we need to be able to listen. We need to be able to listen first with our ears. Our children are talking continuously. I love that about my five kids. They have a knack for all talking at the same time to the same parent and then demanding an answer simultaneously. Even though we put our listening ears on, there's only so much that our human ears can decipher. I know my heavenly Father can decipher it perfectly. If we begin to listen with our ears we may pick up so many things that our children are saying. So what does that look like? It means that we as parents should begin to put aside the cell phone, put aside Facebook, put aside Twitter, put aside Pinterest, put aside the Internet, when our child's voice begins to resonate in our ears, and begin to listen.

I know most parents will laugh at the next scenario because it is so true. I recall one time when my sister was visiting and one of my children called my name. I immediately responded, "Yes, dear," and my sister began to laugh. I asked her, "Why are you laughing at me responding 'Yes, dear' to my child?", and she began to tell me that what I thought was an immediate response was actually delayed by several minutes because my child had actually been calling my name at least 35 times. Now, the 35 times was a bit of an exaggeration, but the point she was making was my child kept saying, mommy, mommy, mommy, mommy, mommy, mommy, mommy, but yet I heard "mommy" just once, and what I thought was an immediate response was actually a delayed response.

Praise God for the insistency of my children that they never give up when they're calling mommy's name, but that taught me a valuable lesson: Get keener at hearing their voice the first time they say "mommy." Can you imagine if your mind and heart were so tuned in to your child that you were that responsive, the type of dialogue and conversation that you can begin to have?

As my oldest girls are now 18 and 13, I am excited when they share different things about their heart. They have learned that when they speak, not only will I listen, but I will covet what they say in a way that I'm guarding their heart and praying for them. I have created a sanctuary of listening, that they feel comfortable being able to share some of their most valuable things; that they trust that within this environment I will be putting aside all things and focusing on them. I have purposefully created that type of environment with each of my children. My husband and I have been intentional about listening to our children with our ears.

The second type of listening that we need to do as parents is to listen with our eyes. That may seem a very odd thing to say, but allow me to elaborate. When you listen with your eyes you're paying attention to the things that your children do not say. Often our children are saying things that are inconsistent with what we are seeing in their behavior. Our child may be walking around moping, but saying with their mouth, "I'm fine." Our child could be hitting a wall, but saying with their mouth, "I'm happy." If their actions and words are inconsistent, then it's our job as a parent to try to find out where the inconsistencies lie and begin to have a conversation with them about how then to become more consistent.

If we begin to listen more with our eyes we will be able to pick up what many researchers say is the most prevalent form of communication, body language. Sometimes people will use body language on a repetitive basis in order to communicate feelings, in order to communicate how they are doing, because sometimes words may escape them. If you were listening to me in an open space where you could visually see me, you will see that I talk with my hands a great deal. I'm a very expressive person with my hands and may even try to paint an entire picture using my hand movement in order to convey my passion about something. Therefore, if you're only listening with your ears you may miss the passion that my body exudes when talking about marriage and family.

Children need someone to listen. When we as parents don't listen, our children will go and find someone who will listen. In most cases, children will find a negative influence that is willing to listen. I have seen through counseling sessions that young girls have found people on the Internet that have taken advantage of them because all they wanted was someone to talk to, and an older man took advantage of that and possibly put them in harm's way. I have seen through other sessions with young boys that they have been victims of gang initiations because they also just wanted someone to listen to them. And because of whatever the case may be the parent or guardian was not available to listen and they went and found someone who would.

I cannot encourage you enough as parents to listen with your heart, listen with your eyes, and listen with your ears.

A B C
ALPHABET SOUP

1. Clear out all clutter. Have a dedicated time each day that you talk with your child and you listen with your ears and your eyes. This means removing all electronic equipment, removing all media, and you as a parent focus on what they are saying.

2. Listen without interruption. Many times we know exactly what we want to say before our child can even finish their sentence. Don't. Let them finish their sentence and then begin speaking. Allow your child to have the opportunity to express themselves and then begin to exhale because now they've gotten it off their chest.

Chapter M

MEDIA

PSALM 101:3a—*I will set nothing wicked before my eyes.*

When our 18-year-old, Alexia, was five years old, she began having difficulties with telling the truth. Like most children, I thought that this was a phase that would change the more that we prayed and talked to her about the consequences of lying. I was wrong. I began to examine her environment and began to understand that there was a television show that she was watching that may have impacted her behavior. The television show was about two brothers who would get into trouble for lying; however, by the end of the show all things worked out. So in the mind of a five-year-old, it was okay to lie because in the end everyone would be forgiven and all would work out.

Again, despite the number of times that my husband and I sat with Alexia and prayed with her and prayed for her, the lying would not stop. As my husband and I went to God in prayer about the type of television shows that she was watching, we began to see patterns of behavior based on different characters that were on television. Of course we were banning the television shows that had mature themes, profanity, nudity, and drugs, but most parents do this. What we failed to do at that time, 13 years ago, was to ban content.

What type of content would be honoring to God that would allow our daughter to flourish? We began to look at TV shows where parents were seen as less than smart and the children were looked at as being more intelligent than the parents. Fast forward 13 years, those TV shows have now taken over the entire wave of television programming for children.

We made a decision 13 years ago to ban certain content from our child. As soon as we stopped her watching the television show and explained the reason why, the lying ceased. It taught us a valuable lesson. God's Word references the eyes on many occasions. What we take in with our eyes filters down to our heart then comes out of our mouth. It is a depiction of what we are digesting. If we want our children to be Christ-focused then we must focus their eyes upon Christ. That may mean turning off the TV in some homes.

It grieves my heart when I hear young children being able to watch R-rated movies and play violent video games. I am not passing judgment upon a parent for doing this, but I'm grieved because the parent doesn't understand the impact that this may have on their child as they are trying to develop a relationship with Christ.

I'd like you, for a moment, to take a survey in your mind of all of the children's television shows that are on the air currently. Walk with me through the themes. Most of the themes revolve around the child being the main character as opposed to the family. The child is usually very intelligent and usually helps solve all of the family dilemmas based on their own antics. In addition, when it comes time for the parents to have lines in the movie or television show, their lines resemble that of an unintelligent person as opposed to that of an intelligent parent. It is only because these shows are comedic in nature, and in order for the laugh track to be at its finest, the parents have to be at their dumbest.

Please don't misunderstand, not every single show on television is this way. However, the vast majority of television shows have started to go this way because of their increasing popularity. Many of my friends will tell me that they allow their kids to watch them because there is no profanity, it's a cute content, and there is nothing else on television to watch.

As I have these dialogues with my friends, I encourage them to think about the content and then the relationship that they have with their own child. If your child has images being placed in their head every single day that they are smarter than you, then the way that they relate to you changes.

There is a proper order in our home. My husband is the head, I am underneath his headship, and the children are thus underneath that authority. If our children think for a minute that the television is right, then what does that say about their knowledge and understanding of God's Word? Did God make an error when He said that the husband should be the head of the household? Are you getting the point? Many times media will have our children question God's Word during a time when they're trying to grow. I think questioning is a good thing and allows for honest dialogue with your child. You are able to take them to scripture and compare what they see with God's standard. However, if they are being exposed to something that you as a parent have said is okay, you've lost your leverage to be able to say "Follow God's Word," when you sit them in front of content that is contrary to God's Word.

I know that this may be a controversial topic, but I want you just to pause for a minute and go through the television shows that your children watch. Then ask yourself, does the content mirror what you are trying to establish in your home. If it does not, you need to make adjustments.

We teach our boys the idea of love and respect for women and their future wives. Likewise, we also teach our girls the idea of submission and respect to their future husbands. On various shows the women are usually more dominant and they're usually the ones that are making most, if not all the decisions. Again, if there's not a correct parental structure within a home, then a child will assume that what they see on a regular basis is the correct way. This causes them to believe that God's Word must be outdated.

Let me clarify an additional point. There are absolutely wonderful single-parent homes. There are absolutely wonderful homes where the grandparents are raising children. Still, the focus should not be deterred from God's original design. It is true that we are living in a society where having a married couple raising children is not the norm; however, that does not mean that we should subscribe to anything that is contrary to God's Word. We still teach God's standard and explain how His grace and mercy allows for variations in the family structure, such as single-parent homes or grandparent homes.

Think about this for a moment. If you were living on a deserted island with just your family and there was nothing to interrupt from the teachings that you give your child, what do you think the outcome would be as far as the importance of the teachings that you give to your child? It may be a farfetched idea, but I hope you get the point. What you are teaching them is going to be the priority because that's all they hear.

So if we take a moment and we turn off our media and we allow our children to hear our voices louder than what media says, then we have a greater opportunity of having our children follows God's Word and not follow the world. God's Word encourages us to be in the world, but not of the world.

Social media has come into our world like a firestorm. Most people are so connected to their social media that we have lost the art of conversation. Social media in and of itself is not a bad thing. However, it can be a bad thing if parents aren't observing where their children are on social media. The same content that I mentioned earlier with television can be the same type of content that they may see with their friends on social media.

Having five children now, we understand the value of monitoring, but yet allowing Internet access at the same time. Allow me to explain. With our 18-year-old, I think that we were far more restrictive on the type of things that she would do when it came to the Internet. With our other children, we have all their passwords, we follow where they go online to ensure that they are properly relaying what they wanted to say while being honoring to God.

We ask them on a regular basis to share their history in cyberspace so we're able to understand where they've gone and why they've gone there. Even with text messaging with the opposite sex, we have had discussions about what is a proper text message to a boy or to a girl, and how that may or may not be edifying to the Lord and to our family.

My children have often shared text messages before sending them to the opposite sex in order to ensure that they are representing themselves as a child of Christ. I am proud of my children in that they don't fight this, as it is a normal part of who we are and how we operate as a family.

A B C
ALPHABET SOUP

1. Survey the television shows that your child watches. Sit down with them and discuss the following:
   - What do they like about the show?
   - Why is the show funny?

- Is there anything in their lives that has caused them to act a certain way towards their siblings or parents? If there is, work with your child to alter their television watching schedule.

2. Take a ride with your child in cyberspace. Review their history on their phone, computer, or tablet and begin to have the same dialogue about what they're viewing and why they're viewing it. I encourage you to be an involved parent, not a distant parent. The more involvement and the more time that you spend with them understanding their world will have positive results, producing a Christ-focused child.

Chapter N

NEW

2 CORINTHIANS 5:17—*Therefore, if anyone is in Christ, the new creation has come: The old is gone, the new is here!*

LAMENTATIONS 3:23—*They are new every morning; great is Your faithfulness.*

You may be wondering why it is that this chapter has two verses. The reason is that there are so many awesome nuggets of information that revolve around the concept of "new" that I could not choose just one. I am surprised that I limited myself to two. The first concept that I would like for you to ponder is the concept that when we or our children accept Christ as our personal Lord and Savior, we become new creations. Because of that all things truly do pass away.

So what does that mean for our children when they accept Christ? What is our obligation as a parent? We are to instruct them to begin life as if they have a new birthday. Think about the celebration that happens when you have a birthday. On that day of your birth you are overjoyed and you are expecting great things to occur. The same can be said when a child accepts Christ. They begin a new life; they have a new birthday, a day that they will now be designated as a Christian.

Far too many times I hear parents continue to define their children based upon old habits or old ways. I remember in my own childhood being told on a repetitive basis that I was certain things that were actually true at the time. As I grew older my parents would sometimes say, well how do we know you've really changed because this is who you used to be. I'm happy to say that because I have accepted Christ as my personal Lord and Savior that those things that I used to be defined as no longer define me, nor hold me captive or hostage. Our children can sometimes feel the same way. If we don't encourage them, that they are truly new creations and new creatures in Christ, who will?

This brings me to my second concept that came from Lamentations. Because God's mercies are new every day we need to make sure as parents that we are wiping the slate clean every day and allowing our children a chance, not only for success, but for failure as well. Far too many times we hold a standard that is so high for our children to achieve that when they fall short—as they often will because they're children—we judge them harshly and don't allow them the opportunity to fail.

Personally, I think it is in my most horrible moments, my most failed attempt at success, that I've had my greatest triumphs and my greatest lessons. Don't rob your children of that. Don't define them by their past, and don't define them by their mistakes. If they make a mistake, use that as an opportunity for growth, attempt to turn it around and have them pray about what God will show them through the adversity, what God will show them through the trials, or what God will show them through the mistakes.

It truly hurts my heart to hear parents criticize their children in the way that I referenced earlier. I've heard parents say to their children that they will never amount to anything because of their father, or they may never amount to anything because they're like their mother. I've also heard parents comment that their children are bad, or their children are horrible. As I cringe to even write these words, I've even heard a mother say, "I wish you were never born." These types of words are damaging to the heart of our children and do not connect them to God's Word. If we're saying to believe everything that is in God's Word, and God's Word says in Lamentations that His mercies are new every day, how can we then hold grudges against our very own children that God has given us to raise for such a time as this?

Allow me to expound on the phrase, "You are bad." When a child hears the phrase that they're bad they begin to internalize that and begin to believe that they, in essence, are a bad person. Now, we may actually be referencing that their actions were bad or the words they used were bad, but sometimes we skip those qualifiers and just go right to you are bad. Therefore, many years later when a child is an adult and they seek counseling from professionals like myself we spend so much time on grappling with the concept that they are not a bad person. Parents, choose wisely the words that you use to convey your disappointment in your children and recognize, just as your Father in heaven has forgiven you, you need to exercise that same forgiveness with your children on a repetitive basis.

I am not implying that you should be a parent that turns a blind eye when there are certain things that are going awry with your child. I fully believe that parents should be holding a child accountable for their actions. God's mercies are truly new with your child every day. You should extend a measure of grace with your child while holding them accountable for their actions. If your child exhibited behaviors that have caused them to be grounded, on punishment, whatever terminology you may use for discipline, you are to awake the next morning with anticipation that their behaviors will be changed because of a heart change. However, you are still holding them accountable for the behaviors the previous day, but with an expectation that because God's mercies are new every day, this is going to be a new opportunity for your child to exhibit positive behavior. Allowing your child to hear the confidence that you have in them because of the God that you both serve will go a long way in modifying and changing your child's behavior.

A B C
ALPHABET SOUP

1. Find ways today to encourage your child. Find ways to remind them of the hidden treasures in God's Word in Lamentations. If God's Word is true, and it is, how are His mercies new every day for your child?

2. Allow your child to make mistakes. Have the type of atmosphere within your home that it's always accepting of mistakes. When mistakes happen use them as an opportunity for growth. Talk to your child about how you and he or she can both grow in whatever the lesson is that God may have presented in front of you.

3. Be transparent. When your child fails, share with them a time in your life when you have had a similar failing or a similar hurt or a similar disappointment, and walk them through what God showed you during that journey. It is amazing what that will do for your child.

Chapter O

OPENNESS

COLOSSIANS 3:9—*Do not lie to one another, since you have put off the old man with his deeds.*

ave you ever heard the phrase, "Do as I say, not as I do"? It is a phrase that has been passed down for generations with regards to raising children. We often tell our children how to follow the right way, but yet we seem to follow a different way. The concept of being open, or even transparent, is something that I don't see that often in our society. I don't see a proper balance of openness and transparency that leads children to make godly decisions, but rather, one of two extremes.

One of the extremes I see is parents keeping secrets about who they were when they were children in order to seem perfect. The other extreme is that parents will act as if their child is their confidante and share every detail of every part of their life, even the things that are inappropriate that would make me blush as an adult. We've seen many Hollywood parents say that they want their children to grow up in such a fashion that there is, "No holds barred." They're saying that their children, even at the ages of 12 and 13, are old enough to handle adult content, where with most kids it would scar them for life.

When I'm writing about openness and transparency, it is being vulnerable to your children to allow them to see what God is doing in your life. It is such a powerful concept, yet very simple. When I think about it, it hits me, "Why am I denying my children information that would be valuable for their adult life?" I have always been a parent that has been open, that has been transparent, but my transparency and openness is truly with a focus upon how will this impact my children in God's kingdom.

My husband and I have purposed in our heart to have the type of marriage that always edifies God and those around us. We attempt to show our children what it's like to be successful, what it's like to have trials, and what it's like to be forgiven in the context of marriage. Bear in mind that our childhoods were vastly different in how our parents communicated. I remember when I was growing up my parents would have arguments in front of us. They didn't teach us how to resolve those conflicts because when they resolved things, that was more in private. My husband, in contrast, would tell me that his parents believed that children should not be a part of adult issues and therefore would have their conversations behind closed doors.

As we understand the dynamics of how we both grew up, we decided to try a different approach. Our approach was that if there was an argument or a disagreement that we would not shy away from having that in front of our children. Let me qualify that by saying there are certain things that our children are not privy to that we do take behind closed doors, but if we're talking about something that causes conflict we would allow that type of disagreement to play out in front of our children. The reason that we do that is because we want our children to understand that conflict is going to happen in marriage, in friendships, in school, at work. The true test of our faith as Christians and our walk is how we deal with and handle the conflict. So what our children see happen, is that we will have a disagreement or have conflict in a certain area, but then they will readily see us resolve that conflict in a manner that is glorifying God.

In addition to that, our openness and transparency also goes with apologies. There are many times that I'm quick to say to my husband that I have wronged you and I am sorry. And on those occasions I publicly declare that in front of my children so that they understand that I have a repentant heart. Repentance means to turn away and not go back to repeat the same behavior, and I make sure that my children understand that my heart is repentant and therefore these are the actions that go along with it, which is an apology to their father.

My husband, likewise, does the exact same thing. He often jokes that sometimes he will "slip up" and punish all five kids for the mistake of one, later to find out that only one child was guilty and then he will have to go back and publicly apologize to the four. In addition, if there is something that he's done within the context of our marriage and he needs to apologize, he will also do that.

So our transparency and openness just doesn't transcend to each other, but it also transcends to our relationship with our children. I would encourage you, as you're reading this book, to also have that type of apology dialogue and fault dialogue that will draw your children closer to Christ because they will be able to seek Him for conflict resolution. Our children see that we make up, we kiss and hug, and then we throw that argument as far behind us as God cast those sins from our past. Then we begin anew and we start that process of walking together towards whatever the goal is that Christ has called us to.

It is not something that happened overnight. We only learned this after several decades of marriage together. We needed to walk in this pathway and make sure that our children understand this type of transparency and openness.

There are times that specifically mothers should address their daughters about behaviors that they may have exhibited that may not be befitting of a wife. God's word instructs the older women to pass on knowledge to the younger women. There have been times when I have not submitted to my husband's authority and decided that I would do things the way I saw fit, only to have God not bless what I was attempting to do. As I have a repentant heart regarding that, I would go to my husband first and apologize, but then I would pull my daughters aside and explain what God's word shares in Ephesians about submission and how there's total freedom and security in that if it's followed correctly. I would explain to them the failings that I had and how to grow from this.

Our children understand that we are not perfect people, but we are people striving towards Christ-likeness in all that we say and do.

A B C
ALPHABET SOUP

1. Admit when you are wrong. This is a very hard process to swallow for some, but admitting that you are wrong will begin to show your children the humanness and the humility that you have before Christ.

2. Apologize when needed. It is imperative that if you have done something to your children in anger, maybe you raised your voice, maybe you disciplined the wrong child, that you go back and make those amends and apologize to that child and allow them to be able to walk with you in a new beginning.

Chapter **P**

PLANTING

JAMES 5:7—*Therefore be patient, brethren, until the coming of the Lord. See how the farmer waits for the precious fruit of the earth, waiting patiently for it until it receives the early and latter rain.*

I recognize that James 5:7 deals with the return of Christ; however, as I read this passage of scripture it reminds me so vividly of our responsibility of planting the right things with our children. I think about this process of a farmer. When you think of a farmer you're automatically led to a person that takes time to find the right soil, to find the right things to plant, to dig down and put those things into the ground, and then to water them on a regular basis and wait to see the fruit that is grown. During that process, the farmer is weeding out all the bad things, and then also allowing for more growth. Wow, what a wonderful picture of what we as parents need to be doing with our children.

Far too many times when we look at our world we see that people are planting things within their home that take root that are damaging. I see many times people are planting bitterness, they're planting destruction, they're planting gossip, they're planting hatred, they're planting laziness. They're planting all the things that are contrary to what God would have children to be; and then we wonder when those things take root in our children, why that has occurred.

I hear the words "generational curse" being used far too many times to describe this process of what God calls planting. Many times I will hear another group of individuals say this family is not able to shake alcoholism or drug addiction because of a generational curse. I will also hear individuals say that there's a long history of incarceration for this family and that has to be a generational curse.

Are we planting the right things within the home to allow for the right type of things to grow? Here's the caveat: You can plant wonderful things all day and still have a bad crop. You could plant bad things all day and still have good things come from the soil. So my point of saying that, is do not misunderstand the words that are contained within this chapter to say that you are not ever able to escape bad planting, or if you have good planting, things will be perfect. That's not what I'm saying. What I hope to convey is that the more consistent we are with the right type of planting, the more consistent our results will then be.

Going back to the analogy of a farmer, imagine as a parent that you begin to plant kindness, you begin to plant Bible study, you begin to plant sacrificial love for siblings; you begin to plant all those type of things in the home. As I mentioned earlier, a farmer digs deep, so you as a family begin to dig down into the fabric and core of who you are as a family and plant those seeds deep. The reason that it's important to dig deep; just like a farmer, if the farmer only puts the seed on the top of the soil, then anything that comes from the elements will wash the seeds away and they won't take root. The same with the family, it is imperative for us to dig a hole that's deep for our family and plant that foundation, that when the storms come the foundation has been planted so deep that we're able to weather the storm as a family. What is that foundation? It is the Word of God.

The next part of planting that's imperative is we begin to water the plants, water the crop. As parents we need to be cultivating. We need to be listening. We need to be loving. We need to be doing all those types of things that I have mentioned in multiple chapters. That's the water that goes on top of the crops. As we're able to take some of those principles from some of those other chapters and put those on top of the crops, then we will eventually over time begin to see the consistent fruit that is born.

Another important element of farming is weeding. When there are things that pop up that are negative to the outcome we begin to pull those things out. Just as a parent, when we start to see negative influences in our child's life we don't just allow the fruit to be spoiled, but instead we pluck out those people and we help them navigate towards people that are more like-minded. We may say birds of a feather flock together; it's the same concept, we're plucking out those things that will not allow our child to achieve what it is that God has intended for them.

Planting takes time. Our society wants to rush through everything. We're ready to just rush the process of planting a seed, watering it, and then watching it grow. Almost like an instant Chia pet. We see with a Chia pet, on the commercial it's that fast; that as soon as you pour the water the hair grows. Nothing in life that has been planted is going to be that quick. Even with a little Miracle Grow, things take time. Therefore, as a parent, we may not see the fruit immediately. Do not be weary; as it says in the beginning of James 5:7, "Be patient." We are to wait in anticipation of what God is doing in that child's life. We are to focus on the type of things that we are planting.

I have said this in many chapters and I will say it again, we have to be careful to look at ourselves first and ask what we are planting in our own lives that have taken root, that have been watered, that are now growing that our children see. If we have picked up horrible habits that our children see have been planted, have taken root and have grown and are now cropping up in our life, it may be hard for our children to be able to see how they are to maintain their own crop, their own fruit as it begins to grow, if they see the contrary happening in our lives.

As I mentioned with that analogy at the beginning, the farmer looks for the fertile ground. This is so imperative for our parenting. If our home is not fertile, nothing will be able to take root. When I mentioned that as parents we need to dig deep and plant those seeds, if the ground is hard and like concrete how will we ever be able to get a seed into the ground? The ground must be fertile. What does that mean? What does that analogy mean for us as Christian parents? It means that our hearts have to be fertile, that we have surrendered our life to Christ and we're asking God to guide us in the way to raise these children. It means that we have created an openness within our home, that God dwells there 24/7. It means that we have removed all elements that will block His existence; that we have set up a structure of accountability in our home that would allow the seeds that we plant to take root upon this fertile ground. All that we do is based upon thus sayeth the Lord in His Word.

You may be asking: Where do I begin? I understand that the ground needs to be fertile, but what do I begin to plant first? The answer is simple: Ask God. What is it that your child needs most right now? Based on the answer, that's what you begin to plant, and that's what you begin to fertilize and to patiently wait to see what God does.

A B C
ALPHABET SOUP

1. Pray about what God would have you plant first. Once God tells you, without delay, PLANT!

2. Examine what you have planted and examine your own harvest and your own crop and determine what weeding needs to take place before you begin to plant for your children.

3. Pray over your children on a repetitive basis with the things that you have purposed in your heart to plant within your home. Begin the process of being a farmer, to patiently wait what God will do in the life of your child.

Chapter Q

QUIET

PSALM 46:10—*Be still and know that I am God.*

The title of this chapter may be very misleading. In no way am I going to teach you how to make your children quiet. What this chapter represents is teaching your children how to find a quiet place with God.

Have you ever noticed how uncomfortable we become when it's silent? If we are out in a restaurant and it becomes too quiet we begin to become paranoid and ask what's wrong, why is it so quiet. Even within our homes, when our children become quiet we always wonder if they're up to mischief. We live in a very loud world, where the silence that can sometimes come across a room can be ominous and threatening at the same time. It is okay to have quiet time. Do you as a parent have quiet time? Do you have a time in which you turn everything off and you just allow God's voice to be the only thing that you hear?

We as parents need to begin to cultivate that type of idea within the minds of your children. In a very fast paced society where we hear the clamoring of so many noises it's imperative that we begin to have a dialogue with our children about what it means to be still and know that God is.

In order for our children to have a vibrant prayer life they need to be able to pick out God's voice as the loudest voice amongst the noise. The only way to begin that process is for them to be quiet, for them to take away all the background noise, take away all the foreground noise and to be able to decipher God's voice amongst all the chatter. Once they're able to do that, then their prayer life will soar.

Often in counseling sessions I give an assignment that deals with being quiet, that deals with the concept of being alone and knowing that God is. I will give the assignment, go to a quiet place and write, whatever the assignment may be. Regardless of whatever the assignment is, many of my clients find that a very intimidating assignment, to go alone and be quiet. Many times they'll come back and say that their house is too loud, they couldn't find a quiet place; or they come back and say that they felt uncomfortable being alone because they're so accustomed to being around people.

This uncomfortable feeling we sometimes have coincides with finding quiet time and hearing God's voice. How can you ever understand His will for your life if you never hear Him speak? How can our children ever understand their purpose if we don't help them understand how God begins to speak to them. In the quietness of the room they should be able to decipher what it is that God would have them do.

We began this process a long time ago with our children by allowing their bedrooms to be a place of refuge and not a place where they would have distractions. Therefore, we purposed in our hearts not to have televisions in any of our children's bedrooms. This was a difficult decision for the children to swallow when it happened; but now, eight years later, they aren't even fazed by it. We have told them that their rooms are a place where they can go and be quiet and know that God will speak to them. Now, they do understand that God doesn't just speak to them in their bedrooms and that He will speak to them anywhere, but at least this is a beginning for them to understand that in the quietness of their room, in the stillness of their room without distraction, they can begin to decipher God's voice from the background noise.

This is so vivid, this idea of being quiet. As it resonates with me I'm thinking about my oldest son who wears bilateral hearing aids. Many times for Alonzo it is extremely difficult for him to decipher between what is background noise and what is noise that is right in front of him. He has had so many success stories of how he's been able to turn off the background noise with his hearing aids and then focus on what is right in front of him and be able to make sense of that. As I think about that analogy with my son, it holds so much truth for us as parents. We need to teach our children how to turn down the volume on what the background noise is and then pay attention to only what is in front of them; focus on what is ahead and be able to hear God's voice as we are quiet in our posture, quiet in our speech, quiet in so many areas of our life that will allow us to be able to hear God's voice.

How loud is your house? Is there a time within your house that you model this for your children? Many adults will tell me that they feel uncomfortable coming in and having their house quiet. They may not even watch television, but they purposely will turn the TV on to have, as they call it, background noise, because it makes them comfortable. Are you able to turn down the volume of the background noise in your own home so that you will be able to hear God's voice? If you begin to exercise this you will be able to show your child what it's like to hear God's voice. They in turn will be able to turn down the background noise and do the same.

A B C
ALPHABET SOUP

1. Create a quiet place for your child. We removed all televisions from our children's bedrooms and that seems to have worked for our family. It may work for yours, but it may not. Find a place that your child can take refuge to be able to have a time of being alone with God, a time to just hear His voice, create their prayer closet.

2. Model finding quiet time and hearing God's voice for your children. You and your spouse need to do this as a duo to show that even mom and dad can get away, be alone and hear God's voice.

3. Model for your child what it looks like to act when you hear. Much like a child, when a child is instructed to do something after they have heard their parents' desires and wishes or commands, the child immediately goes into action. Show your child what that looks like as God begins to talk to you in the quietness. Show your child what it looks like to immediately hear and immediately obey. This type of walk for your children, and transparent state, will shape who they are.

Chapter R

READING

PSALM 119:105—*Your word is a lamp to my feet and a light to my path.*

Our family loves to listen to all types of music. One of our favorite genres is Christian rap. There's an artist who wrote a song titled *LeVar*.[1] The song indicates that LeVar Burton, the host of *Reading Rainbow*, told generations upon generations how important reading was, but instead the generations focused on secular things other than reading, and the Christian rap artist then goes on to say that we are where we are based on that.

It is a song that my children listen to quite often and discuss as a family. We also talk about the value of reading. There are two types of reading that I would like to explore during the time we have together in this chapter. The first, which is the most important, is the reading of God's Word.

In the scripture passage noted above, God reminds us how important His Word is; that it is truly a lamp to our feet and a light to our path. Take a moment to understand, that as you digest God's Word it becomes an illumination to everywhere you go. Therefore, you won't walk in darkness when you have properly digested God's Word. What do I mean by properly digest it? We can't take scripture passages out of context. I often hear people quote the famous Ephesians 5 passage about women being submissive; however, we lose the context in which God calls us first to submit to Him, and then there is a relationship that occurs with that, wives willingly aligning themselves underneath the husband's authority.

We like our favorite Bible verses, but then we pull away from those that may be convicting; we decide only a part of God's Word applies to us. I used to think that this was because we were at a "buffet" and we decided to pick and choose. As I have grown in my faith I have come to understand that there is a lack of reading of God's Word that would then translate into a lack of understanding. If we would only take the time to read God's Word on a repetitive basis then we would begin to unlock some of the truths that His Word has for us.

Take, for example, your owner's manual in your vehicle. If you were only to read how to turn your lights on and how to make sure that the key comes out of the ignition without damaging anything, you would miss the connection between that key and how to turn the vehicle on. You'd also miss the connection between the lights and how the lights being left on may drain the battery. You would miss the connectivity of all the parts of your vehicle based on your limited reading.

As I have discovered this, I am now less apt to judge a person when they only pull certain parts of scripture and apply it to their life. I want to encourage that person to go look at scripture in its totality. When I was a new Christian and young in my faith I only had an arsenal of a few verses. Therefore, I based everything in my life just on those few verses that I memorized and hid in my heart. What I realized, is that as I grew in my walk and my "milk" turned to something meatier, I now have a bigger arsenal from which to pull from. My toolbox overflows with things that God has given to me to be able to use on a repetitive basis.

This toolbox needs to be given to our children. Your child is never too young to learn how to read God's Word. We never know what may resonate inside them during the time they begin reading God's Word. It truly is amazing to watch a two or three-year-old repeat after you as you read God's Word. I would suggest that even if you are pregnant as you are reading this book, or have a very new baby, begin to allow God's Word to be a lullaby to the ears of your unborn child or to your newborn infant. There is such a soothing calm feeling that comes over children as they're bathed in the Word of God.

If your child understands that that book, that Holy Book can change their life and should be deemed as the most important book they'll ever read, they then will take it more seriously. There's one problem with trying to implement that. Can you guess what I am about to say? If you don't take it seriously, and if you are not in your Bible the way you should be, then your child will not. Remember, all throughout this book I have said that everything that you do, your child does in triplicate. Therefore, if you value God's Word above all other books then you are showing your child how to live properly and how to navigate through many of life's challenges.

I've heard some people complain that God's Word for children is sometimes too difficult to understand. God even tells us if we don't understand, to ask. Therefore, prior to reading God's Word with my children I have them pray individually that God will begin to open their eyes, open their hearts and open their ears as they hear God's Word and they digest what they need for that time. Every single time they pray that God will open up something new that they didn't see before.

There should be a regular time of Bible study within your home. Whether or not you have the capacity within your schedule to do it on a daily basis, there should be minimally a weekly study of God's Word that shares and shows the importance to your children of how to use God's Word in our world today. Regardless of whether you can do a full Bible study on a daily basis, you need to be in scripture with your child every day. If there is a verse that you can give them that they can read prior to leaving the home, do that.

I mentioned before in this book that every room in our house is filled with scripture. I want to be clear that even though scripture is written on the walls wherever you look that doesn't take away from the actual opening of the Bible and the actual going through the pages and allowing your child to see God's Word resonate from the pages.

I am a big techie person and my Bible is actually on my iPad. However, as my children are growing and learning the Bible I want them to have the rich experience of going through an actual Bible in their hand that is not an electronic version. I want them to see how carefully God has laid out the pages and how He has orchestrated each of the chapters to follow one after another in succession. Therefore, our children have their own individualized Bible with their name that they can flip through and they can write in. Of course as they get older, when they are in high school, we give the option of having an electronic version to accompany their hardcopy version. To my amazement, our oldest daughter, who is a college student, still does not use an electronic version that she goes to as a first line of reading. She still pulls out her tattered Bible that has been taped and glued in some places.

It is imperative that you as a parent read God's Word in front of your children. It is imperative that they read God's Word. One of our favorite times as a family in the previous years has been just to allow each of the children to find a Bible passage that they like and read it before we have evening prayer. That has been a rich time in our lives that has allowed our children to be able to feel that they are contributing to the spiritual growth of our family.

Early in the chapter I mentioned there were two types of reading that I wanted to discuss with you. The second type of reading is reading for educational purposes, for academia. Many times we think that academic excellence through reading is not necessary in order to attain good jobs or achieve a certain status that God would have for you in a company. I disagree. Reading provides such a strong foundation for you in all learning. Did you realize that your local newspaper, be it online or hard copy, most of your books and magazines, are written at a fifth or sixth grade reading level? The reason being is that the reading level of most adults has diminished over the years due to a lack of reading. Our society has stopped promoting the reading of classic literature in some schools. We've stopped reading so many different books. We've stopped reading and we rely on more visual cues.

There is such a richness of knowledge and learning that helps with growth if you take the time to immerse your children in reading. During the summer months when our children are out of school, we do not believe in just having a summer vacation free of education. Our children read all summer long and they have workbooks that they complete all summer long. It is great to see that their test scores reflect that as they head back to school. Their teachers have been complimentary of the fact that they never lose any of the knowledge from the previous year and in fact sometimes grow further past where they were at the beginning of the summer.

One of the tasks that we give our children is not only to read, but to comprehend. They are allowed to go to our local bookstores and purchase as many books as they would like to read during the summer. Then after each chapter they write a summary of what the chapter was about, and then by the end they have a book report several pages long based on the chapters. We allow the books to be based upon their reading levels of course, and interests. We want them to enjoy reading and to stay focused and occupied during what seems to be academia downtime.

The more knowledge your child has and the more worlds they can visit through a book, the better they will be equipped to deal with many life situations. This is something that we have done from the time our children were little, to pour into them the importance of reading multiple books and different mediums of expression, whether it be a hardcover book, a paperback, an audio book or something that's an electronic version.

As I stated in the introduction of this book, our oldest daughter was valedictorian of her senior class and worked very hard to achieve that status. I truly believe that the emphasis that we had on reading and attaining knowledge through several different types of books aided in her achievement of the valedictorian status.

Reading should never be a chore. It should be something that your children enjoy. In our family, our boys did not enjoy reading as much as the girls. To be transparent, they still don't. As a matter of fact, it was a struggle at times to get our boys to even read. There was a method to the madness of having them do a summary after each chapter they read. I found that sometimes my boys were zooming through books and then I would ask questions about the content and they would shrug their shoulders and say I don't remember. Therefore, we implemented that little strategy of written chapter reports to avoid a lack of comprehension.

What I found with my boys is that I had to find books that captured and piqued their interest. I would spend hours at Barnes & Noble with different staff people asking them about different books that would pique the interest of my children, especially my boys. They would often ask me, what type of things do your sons enjoy doing, and as I would give them a list of those things they would find books that most often fit their personality and their reading style.

I also had the challenge as a parent to make sure that the content was appropriate. Being that it was Barnes & Noble, it wasn't a Christian bookstore, so there could have been messages or images within those books that I had to ensure were appropriate for a Christian child. Therefore, in many cases I would sit in Barnes & Noble and read the book to make sure that it was appropriate. In most cases I wasn't able to read the book in its totality, but I was at least able to do some review of the book and read maybe one chapter to ensure that the content was not contradicting anything that we had in our home.

As you see, this is an area that we have spent a lot of time as parents making sure that we are pouring into our children, but pouring into them correctly.

A B C
ALPHABET SOUP

1. Read the Bible. You as a parent must make sure that you are visibly reading your Bible in front of your child to show the importance and value you place on God's Word.
2. Read the Bible with your child. Make sure they see that you want to be involved in their spiritual growth by reading the Bible with them.
3. Give them a reading assignment out of the Bible. Give them a Bible study to do. Ask them to journal about what God's Word says to them in a certain area.
4. Have them lead prayer with their favorite Bible verse. Have them talk about what that Bible verse means.
5. Lastly, from an academic standpoint, read, read, read. Make sure that you find books that will pique your child's interest. Make sure that you are able to link them in with a book

club within your local library. Every summer most libraries will have a book club that your child can join. This is a great opportunity to advance their education. Continue to have them read everything that you can, from cookbooks, to signs on the highway. Continue to increase their educational level.

Chapter 5

SIBLINGS

EPHESIANS 4:32—*Be kind to one another, tenderhearted, forgiving each other, just as God in Christ has also forgiven you.*

ave you ever heard this: He's touching me. No, I'm not. Yes, you are. He touched me first. She touched me first. And then finally mom or dad exclaims: Everyone, keep your hands to yourself.

If you haven't heard this, chances are you have an only child. Most often I hear this as we are driving to and from school, to and from church, to and from soccer, to and from basketball, ballet, crochet ministry. Okay, I hear it everywhere. Any place you can think of, I have to be the referee with sibling rivalry.

It is an absolute joy to have five children that absolutely love each other and absolutely can't stand to be away from each other. At the same time, they absolutely get on each other's nerves simultaneously. It is healthy when siblings are able to have an argument that they are able to navigate through with parental advisement. I'm not advocating a

Cain and Abel type of rivalry, but rather I'm advocating that if children learn within the context of their own home to "fight fairly" and "argue fairly," then they will be able to transfer those same types of skill sets into other relationships as they grow older.

It truly saddens my heart as I hear in society that many people do not like their siblings or do not get along with their siblings for whatever reason. It could be jealousy. It could be family bitterness. It could be money issues, but for whatever reason we see many sibling splits. We see them in Hollywood. We see them in our own families. We see them in movie scripts. We see them in so many ways, that siblings may not get along and decide to never communicate with each other moving forward.

As we have raised our five children we have instilled in them that they are a family even outside of mom and dad. In fact, just this morning I was explaining to my nine-year-old son Avery that one day mommy and daddy will no longer walk the earth with them, God may call mommy at one time and may call daddy at another time to come home and be with Him and at that point the five children that are left are to continue the legacy that mommy and daddy have started. It may seem morbid to have that type of conversation with a nine-year-old, but in fact we've had this conversation with each of our children from the time that they were able to understand our voice. We want them to know that God has called our family for a purpose. God has called our family to impact His kingdom and be an impact family. In order to do that the family unit, including the siblings, have to be intact. It doesn't mean perfect, but it does mean striving towards that which is connected.

We tell our children continuously that they should love one another. We teach them from Ephesians 4:32 that God says to be kind to your siblings, to be tenderhearted towards your siblings, to forgive your siblings. And why should they do these things; because God in Christ has forgiven them. So if we're able to have them understand the concepts in that verse, then being with each other becomes easier.

Most recently a young woman at our church gave our family a compliment, stating that the kids are so happy and she's never seen children that enjoy being around each other. I had to laugh, because only moments before, there was a fight amongst the siblings about who stole something out of another person's room. I praise God for what that outward appearance looked like, as we have worked so hard on the inside. We have gone through so many different arguments and so many different conversations to all end up in the same place. We end with teaching our children to love one another no matter what.

Although this may sound like a very simple concept, sometimes we've had to employ actual behavioral strategies to help change the hearts of our children in reference to one another. My husband came up with a brilliant idea many years ago called the good deed chart. We started to see our children arguing over simple things that weren't worth arguing over. We saw them being selfish with certain things and not sharing with one another and not looking out for each other. Again, as I referenced before, we have taught our children over and over that once we are gone they will have the responsibility of caring and looking out for one another. Therefore, it's imperative for us to begin to teach that process as they are young. As they grow older, it is just part of who they are and what they've become.

I love the fact that I look in my family, and I look in my husband's family, and I see this generational concept of caring for one another. My mother's family is a very close-knit family, the Bogees. Any time an event, good or bad, happens within the Bogee family, despite the fact that they are spread out as far as Hawaii to New York, every sibling knows immediately, and every sibling begins to call on the phone to inquire about their sibling or even their sibling's children.

I also love, in my husband's family on both sides, the Parhams and the Whites, that there is a deep love and caring for each other. Fortunately, I have been adopted into both the Parham family and the White family, as not an in-law, but truly a daughter. I have been able to see the type of love and caring that the sibling sisters and brothers have for one another on both sides of the family. It is that type of love and caring that we try to show our children, that we are trying to foster in them.

Therefore, going back to the good deed chart, it was a way to foster selfless acts of love amongst our children. My husband created a chart that had each child's name with 20 boxes following their name. When we observed one of the children doing a "good deed" for another, we would give them a star. Once their 20 boxes were filled with stars they were able to have a special surprise that daddy would go and purchase for them. It would be definitely something worth earning.

Interestingly, as the good deed chart was implemented we began to see that they were very conscious of their actions, and sometimes they would purposely do things in order to get a star. Therefore, just like all good behavioral plans, you have to alter the plan to fit the current situation. So we began to alter the chart and tell them it had to be genuine, we are not giving a star for a purposeful act and you cannot ask to have a star placed in your box based on something that you did. In fact, my husband told them that if they pointed out what they did to earn a star, he would take one away. My children tried every way possible to earn those stars while staying within the rules. The good deed chart finally transitioned into something that was more selfless and focused on the sibling. Eventually they began to do things for one another without even remembering there was a good deed chart. They were able to transition to being selfless individuals with their siblings and looking out for one another in such a positive and impactful way. I do want to add that they are still a beautiful work in progress and need gentle reminders.

After a few years of implementing the good deed chart we recognized that the two brothers were not being as kind to each other as they possibly could. So my husband came up with the "Show Brotherly Love" chart. This chart was the exact same type of idea as the good deed chart, housed right underneath the good deed chart, but dealt with showing brotherly love. I find it comical that most often our children would say to each other, particularly the boys: I don't think that you're going to earn a star on the brotherly love chart today. It encouraged the brothers to begin to look at just not doing good things for their sisters, but also doing good things for each other.

The girls often laughed that sometimes the boys' brotherly love chart was completely empty for weeks on end. But as soon as they would point that out they would become conscious of their behavior and then begin to have stars put on their brotherly love chart. To this day this is something that we still do. It is not a focal point anymore as it used to be, posted in the middle of the kitchen for all to walk by and see, but it is something now that is engrained in them that they are to continue to do until God calls us all home.

God has blessed me with two siblings whom I love dearly, Matthew John and Marjory. I recall growing up with them, being the oldest sibling, knowing that there was a sense of responsibility that I had to look out after them. If you were to ask my sister, I was probably meaner than what she would have probably wanted and did less looking out for her than what I probably should have. Having siblings teaches us the idea of cooperation within a society; it teaches us the idea of brotherhood and fellowship within a society. Being a big sister has caused me to grow immensely in several areas.

Your home becomes a microcosm of society; therefore, having multiple siblings means having multiple personalities to get along with.

Having that sacrificial love for your brother or your sister translates into being more tolerant of your coworkers on the job. It may mean being able to be more sensitive to the needs of your friends. You learn how to be a friend, since your siblings are your first friends. It also may mean being more tolerant of a difficult boss that God may have placed in your path because you have learned how to deal with a difficult sibling issue.

Therefore, there is such great value in having multiple children. Just not for your child to have someone to play with, but to also begin to teach them some of those valuable lessons of how to deal with people.

I have spoken on the importance of strengthening sibling relationships within the home, but how do we do that outside of the home? One of the key areas in which we have done this is that we encourage our children to support their siblings in whatever area that are important to them. For example, both of our sons are athletes. We make a point of ensuring that the siblings go to each other's athletic events. For our youngest son Avery who plays soccer, we attempt to schedule family soccer outings to ensure that we are there in support. The children yell and cheer each other on. They are the biggest cheerleaders on the sidelines for their siblings.

As my oldest son plays basketball, we will alter the family activities to ensure that we all can attend. Having a big family doesn't mean that we're able to successfully navigate our schedule 100 percent of the time, but we try to make a point of doing that as often as possible.

A B C
ALPHABET SOUP

1. Within your home try to find activities that all siblings can learn to do together. Whether it's a board game, a video game,

a book study, have them pick out activities that they will, in cooperation, do together.

2. Make a calendar of all of the activities that your children are involved in outside of the home. Ask the siblings to choose which of those activities that they will attend and commit to on a regular basis.

3. Begin to have your children pray for one another. As they begin to pray for their brother or sister it becomes harder to argue with them. Have them to commit to praying for their siblings on a regular basis.

Chapter T

TEACH

PROVERBS 22:6—*Train up a child in the way he should go, and when he is old he will not depart from it.*

One day my children and I went through a car wash. This is a typical occurrence as many of the roads around our subdivision are dirt roads and oftentimes our van ends up very dirty. On this occasion I recall saying to the kids, "Why do you think a car going through a car wash is like being a sinner?" Several of my children raised their hand and said, "Ooh, mommy, mommy, mommy, I know, I know the answer." As we're going through the car wash, my sweet middle daughter Alyssa explained that a car going through a car wash and a sinner are very similar because you come to Christ dirty and as you come out on the other side you're very clean. I chuckled and I said, exactly. Will you ever see a car wash the same again? Years later as we go through a car wash our kids are still saying this reminds me of what it means to become clean and knowing Jesus Christ as your personal Lord and Savior.

I share that story for you to understand that every moment, absolutely every second of being a parent, is a teachable moment. God has only given you a brief amount of time to be with your children, so use every moment to your advantage to teach them.

I often ask myself, what is the legacy that I will leave behind through my teaching? If I were in heaven and I were glancing at my children after leaving them, what evidence of my teaching would I be able to see being borne in their lives? As I look at many of the movie stars that are on television or on the big screen, I am sad because many of the behaviors that they exhibit that are counterproductive or dangerous or detrimental are displayed with their own children. Many times you see history repeating itself based on the parents' life choices.

I won't name any names, but I'm sure that if you took a moment and thought about patterns of behaviors that you see people exhibit in society that have been passed down negatively to their children, I'm sure you can think of more than just a few. What we exhibit, either through our mouths or through our actions, is passed down. Teaching is not always in a formal classroom. Teaching is through our behavior. Teaching is through our language. Teaching is through our attitudes. Teaching is through our prayer life. Teaching is through our Bible study. What are you teaching your children as they are observing you?

Every moment that we go out into the world I look at it as an opportunity for me to begin to share with my children how God has given me a love for people to evangelize. When we are at restaurants I often engage wait staff in a friendly manner, so much so that my children tease me when a waiter or waitress comes over, that mom is going to talk this person's ear off, and will continuously laugh as I thank them with gratitude for their service. At the end of our meal I often will leave a tract that is wrapped within the bill. I want them to know about the love of Jesus. I want them to understand the kindness of Christians and the gratitude of Christians, and then at the end of that meal share why we may be set apart and why we may be different.

My children see this on a repetitive basis, and even though sometimes it's funny to them and to my husband, that mom just thanks everyone for every single thing, it is a valuable lesson that I know they will hold within their heart and continue to use as they grow older.

If we are out in the community, I make my children pay attention to those who are around them. If there are older individuals and we are seated, my boys immediately stand up and offer their seat. If there's a pregnant woman, my boys will immediately offer their seat. If there's even a female with children, my boys will immediately offer their seat. It's amazing to me how many people are amazed that those types of old-fashioned values are still being taught to children. My husband has made sure that our boys are growing up to be godly men with godly character. And that is not something that can just be told, but it's something that they witness him do, therefore the teaching starts with his own actions. I also recognize that my husband has instructed or taught our boys to care for me and to care for their sisters when he is not around. In a loving way they are very protective of their sisters and of their mother.

Much like my husband's teaching of the boys, I do the same teaching with the girls. I teach them many things of being quiet in spirit but still being loud in action. I help them balance that out so they can be heard as a woman in society, where sometimes we are forgotten about and sometimes we are not treated fairly.

There are many lessons that my parents taught me based on their work ethic and based on their actions that I will forever hold dear. I love being involved in every field trip possible with my children. I contemplate where that has come from, and it has come from the teaching that my mother Lydia Alston instilled in me as a little girl. Again, it wasn't anything that she said, but it was by her actions that she taught. My mother worked in various emergency rooms, including those affiliated with Veteran's Administration hospitals, as a respiratory therapist. My mother truly is the hardest working woman that I have ever met. She would tirelessly work several shifts, either midnights or days, but would always find time for her children. No matter how big or how small the field trip was, my mother would arrange her work schedule in such a way that she was always present at every field trip.

Honestly, when those things would occur as a child, I didn't understand the gravity of what that meant. In fact, oftentimes I was annoyed as I got older in high school. I remember a church youth group outing to Cedar Point in Ohio one year, while I was in tenth grade. We were living in Indiana at the time, and because it would be a long trip my mother could not go. I was so excited because this was my first outing without my mother. I had arranged my seat so that I could sit next to the cutest boy on the bus. The bus started to pull out of the parking lot and then abruptly stopped. The bus driver opened the bus doors and in walks, you guessed it, my mother. She arranged to have the next two days off so that she would be able to go. Imagine my excitement.

As an adult having my own children, I recognize the sacrifice that my mother had to make in order to rearrange her work schedule to be at every field trip. What that taught me was that I was important enough to change anything in her life to be a part of even the smallest portions of my day. That left such an imprint in my heart that I'm forever grateful for my mother being able to do that for me.

Therefore, I do the exact same thing with my children. I attempt to make it to every single field trip because I want them to also have that same imprint upon their heart of how important it is to me to want to be involved in every aspect of their life. I'd never want to be a mother that sits at home or work and cheers, but I want to be at the game with them cheering them on.

I reflect on the teachings of my father, Matthew Alston. As we grew up it was frustrating to me that he wanted to keep our house so clean and so organized. Every moment of every day it seemed there was a focus on cleanliness. However, I have to admit that I am an exact carbon copy of my father in that area. It gives me joy and relaxation to walk into a home that is organized and clean. The benefit that teaching has had for me as an adult is that having a big family has been easier for me only because there is this type of organization. Having a home that is organized has served my children well. They're able to come in and be comfortable within their home. They're able to come into their home and have a place that's set aside for them, that they're able to do their homework, be able to comfortably entertain friends, and have our home be a place where people can come and it's a place of refuge.

If someone is hurting and they walk into our home, I don't want them to walk into our home and see chaos, but I want them to see, just like God in His Word is a God of order and not confusion, my home should represent the same. So I'm sure that my children have that same annoyed look that I did as a child when I ask them to pick up after themselves. It truly is to honor God and is truly another way to teach them.

A B C
ALPHABET SOUP

1. Every moment is a teachable moment, whether you're cooking, cleaning, driving; every moment that you have with your child is an opportunity for you to teach them something about themselves, about you, or about their Creator.

2. Find one teachable moment every single day. As you begin to find that one teachable moment every single day, you will see them glaring in front of you in the subsequent days to come.

3. Walk your children through your own childhood experiences and what your family taught you. Whether your experience was good or bad as a child, there's always something that God was teaching you. Where the childhood was unbearable, God may have taught you endurance. If your childhood was ecstatically joyful, God may have been teaching you how to pass that down to another generation. Find different ideas from your own childhood that you can begin to sow into your children.

Chapter U

UNIQUE

LUKE 12:7—*Indeed, the very hairs of your head are all numbered. Don't be afraid; you are worth more than many sparrows.*

Isn't it amazing that God has numbered the hairs on your head? He knows every detail of your life. It gives me such comfort knowing that my heavenly Father knows every intricate detail about my life and then is a parent to me based on that relationship.

Sometimes during counseling sessions I have been the one to inform parents about what their child likes or dislikes. Many times within the walls of that counseling session a child's uniqueness is apparent based on their language, their body language, the things that they gravitate toward or their friendships, but many times parents miss the boat on those type of subtle cues.

During counseling sessions I always encourage parents to find the uniqueness about each individual child. Just as God has created us like beautiful snowflakes, there are no snowflakes that are found that are

114

alike. There is not one person on this earth that is like your child. We may joke as parents now, that our mother or father said one day you will have a child just like you, but in essence it may be akin to the behaviors that they have, not necessarily your carbon copy. Even when we say someone is the spitting image of another, it is not to say that they are truly identical in any way.

It is amazing that we have an opportunity to find what makes our child tick. It doesn't matter if you have one child, or if you have five like we do; your job as a parent is to first find out what makes the child unique, and then secondly, try to come alongside them, as God's Word encourages us to do as believers, and help draw that uniqueness out for the purpose that God has intended.

I love knowing that each of my five children had different tickle spots as babies. Even though I have a set of twins, each of them had a different area on their neck that was the one little area that they would love for mommy and daddy to tickle. There are certain areas that are still those sensitive tickle spots even as they grow. They may not be literally a tickle spot, but it may be that unique part of them that is so different that only a mother or father can know based on a relationship.

Throughout much of this book I have talked about coveting time with your child and pouring into them and learning about them.

I remember the pastor at my oldest daughter's church saying that husbands should have a Bachelor's, Master's, and Ph.D. in their wives. I would agree that the same should be held true for children. You should study your children so astutely that you should have a Ph.D. in your child. Here's the interesting thing. The Ph.D. in that child is going to be different than the Ph.D. that you may hold for another child. I cannot emphasize enough that each child has been created uniquely.

I sometimes wonder if my twins really are twins. God has created them so uniquely different. Alonzo is very outgoing, very social, and laughs continuously, where his twin Alyssa is very reflective and quiet and has a soft spirit. The only way that my husband and I would know this is because we spend time getting to know who they are.

Can you imagine the comfort that your child has knowing that, aside from God, you know them better than anyone on earth? Even as adults we can look back and know without a shadow of a doubt that our parents had that relationship with us, if it was a good relationship, where they understood and knew our uniqueness.

Sometimes the uniqueness of a child goes against the grain of society. There are children that are raised in homes where everyone is an athlete, but one musically gifted child. Instead of celebrating that difference, we may question why they can't be like the rest of the family. Praise God for the diversity that can be found within a family. I'm excited to walk this path with my five children and continuously discover new things about them every day.

I've been married for almost 23 years and every day being with my husband there are new things that I discover. The reason that I discover new things about him and my children is that as we draw closer to Christ and we become more Christ-like, we begin to change. Those things that used to be important to the inner man are no longer apparent to us. We begin to look different, to talk different, to act different. The decisions that we made yesterday are not the decisions that we make today.

One of our most common prayers in our family is, Lord, help me be a better Christian today than I was yesterday. And if that's true, and if we are striving to do that, then you would be a unique person every single day.

A B C
ALPHABET SOUP

1. Make a list of all the different characteristics that make your child unique and find a way to celebrate each characteristic. Let them know that being different and being unique is God's design. Have them celebrate with you their uniqueness.

2. Have each sibling compliment their siblings on the uniqueness that they hold within the family. Definitely have a time of sharing and growing amongst siblings to find those things that are most unique.

3. Try to celebrate when there are differences that come about on a daily basis. As I stated earlier, we evolve daily as we are growing closer to Christ; therefore, that uniqueness that God has given us changes.

4. Be a student of your child and study them to understand how God has uniquely gifted them.

Chapter **V**

VALUE

MATTHEW 6:21—*For where your treasure is, there your heart will be also.*

hat is it that you value as an individual? Most often you will see your child emulate those same things. I remember a friend years ago who loved clothing and loved shopping. She only would spend money on the most expensive designer clothing. Her whole paycheck would most often be used to find the most expensive items to purchase. Years later God blessed her with a daughter and that daughter followed suit in the same mind-set that her mother had, with designer clothing being a value.

I'm not implying that there's anything wrong with designer clothing. I do love my designer handbags. However, my value and worth is not placed within those things to where it passes on to my children and they make those things valuable.

From your conversations and your actions your children will know exactly the things that you value in your heart and hold true. The things that you value are typically those things that you become most passionate about; those things that you will spend valuable time doing. The value that you place in every area of your life is evident to your children.

Our society has often placed value on money and status. We see this through many of the secular songs that are sung by many artists. Whether it's R&B, hip-hop, country, contemporary, we see a theme regarding the acquisition of items. We hear singers sing about using money to get a girl, a guy; using money to get a big house, a nice car, fancy clothing or fur coats. We see this whole concept of our society valuing things. When there is a shift in the song, where we are hearing ballads or love songs, then we see there's a value that's placed on people; still not the right value. But most often we see our young children, young adults listening to more of the songs that place a value on the acquisition of things. Recently, I have a heard a shift in some gospel songs that falsely teach that God wants us all to have riches and you should just claim it and it will be yours.

How important is acquiring things to you as a parent? What type of things do you place your value in and how is that evident to your children? Are you placing value in your time spent with God? If your children were to be asked the question, "What is the most important thing in mommy or daddy's life," what do you think their answer would be? Why not ask them as you're reading this book. If they give an answer such as your television show, your iPad, your iPhone, your car, your job, then it's time to readjust your focus and begin to look at ways to change that.

The way to change that is not to simply start focusing on something else, but the way to change it is through prayer, that God will take the desires for worldly things, or the desire for things that distract you from where He wants you to be and place your value upon those things that

He has called you to value. If you simply just shift your eyes you still haven't shifted your heart. Matthew 6:21 says that where your treasure is, there your heart will be also. We also know through God's Word, that as the things that are in your heart are implanted there, it flows through your mouth, and so your language even changes when your heart begins to change.

If you become obsessed with talking about technological things, or you become obsessed with talking about fast cars or TV shows, that's an indication as to where your heart is; therefore, those things that are in your heart flow through your mouth. It doesn't even have to be an obsession or fetish over things, but maybe there's a constant focus on those things.

I'm not saying that it's bad to place desires or likes upon certain things. I am probably one of the biggest techie people around and have to have every possible Mac product that there is to have. I love gadgets; and yes, I will spend time speaking with others about gadgets, and my children probably would list my gadgets in one of my top ten areas. However, my gadgets will never take the top spot. I hope I am getting the difference across, that it is okay to like certain things, but you should never value things.

As couples have come into marital counseling with me this has been an area of contention for some. Their values have drifted apart. Whereas when Christian couples have come together in marriage their value was placed upon God who brought their union together and they ascribe to Ecclesiastes 4, which references a threefold cord, and knew that God was that strand that was in the middle that held them together and not apart. As they began to experience jobs and life and children, the outside world began to trickle in and the threefold cord began to fray and their values, in their eyes, began to shift to other things, then the marital issues began to happen. Many times in marital counseling we're doing a value evaluation and determining what are the things that you value most and how do we get back on track, how do we put those pieces of the marriage back together so that their value systems are on the same page.

I cannot stress enough that your children emulate everything that you do. If your children do not understand the things that you value, then it's time for you to be in prayer to change that.

How do you get your children to begin the process of placing proper value in certain areas of their life? You encourage them to fix their eyes upon God and ask them to begin to pray about those things that God would call them to change and to do within their own life. Through this process of becoming who God wants them to be, certain areas will be placed in front of them that will cause their value system to shift and change in a positive way. There are so many different ways that your children will be able to walk through this process.

A B C
ALPHABET SOUP

1. Fix your own value systems so that the things that you value trickle down to your children in a positive way.

2. Help your children seek God's face first in order to develop a value system that will lead them to be a productive child in the kingdom of God.

Chapter **W**

WORSHIP

PSALM 150:6—*Let everything that has breath praise the LORD. Praise the LORD!*

Are you familiar with the group called the Jackson 5? Well, our family has been called the White 5. We absolutely love to praise and worship God in any setting possible. All five of our children are musically gifted. They all play the piano and some sing. A few play multiple instruments, such as the drums, bongos, guitar, melodica, to name a few. When we hear the words resonating from God's script, "Let everything that has breath praise the LORD. Praise the LORD," we just want to shout it to the ends of the earth and use music as a way to express our worship.

In what ways does your family express worship? We love to express our worship through music all throughout our home. The front room in our house has a piano and on the walls of that room are scripture passages from the book of Psalms that remind us to praise God with loud sounds, to praise Him in every way possible. We love to gather in that front room to hear the piano and drums and guitar playing and just sing about our love for God. It is such a wonderful time of worship for our family because it's a time when we can forget about everything that's on the outside and just focus our praise on an audience of One. When we leave out of that room collectively as a family we feel energized. We feel that we are able to conquer the world and the world's kryptonite won't bother us because we've just been connected as a family singing praises and worshipping God.

There are so many ways that we see worship being manifest in the day in which we live. Sometimes that word "worship" means something in a negative connotation. We sometimes think of the word worship when it comes to idols. We ask ourselves, what is it that we worship? It reminds me very much of the chapter that dealt with values: Where is your heart's treasure and what do you value? The same can be said in this chapter for worship: Where do you find yourself spending the most time? What type of activities cause you to be with or without your family, good or bad? Are there certain things that you worship? Are there certain people that you worship? If your worship is something other than the Lord God Almighty, then it's time to fix your focus, as my close friend Cheryl McKinney would say.

It is so easy to have our eyes become fixed on things that become idols. I recall several years ago that I had to fix my focus. I recall spending more time searching the threads on Facebook than I did searching the threads in the Bible. I was very interested in what my family and friends and coworkers were doing on Facebook. I was not focused on what God wanted me to see first. So I purposed in my heart that I would fix my focus and worship only one God and not God and Facebook. I made a commitment at that time that I would not be allowed to be on Facebook, or any social media for that matter, if I had not spent a sufficient amount of time daily with the Lord.

I have to be honest that it was not as easy a task as it sounds. Because I had conditioned myself to be so linked to social media to find out who, what, when, where and why, taking the time to prioritize God, what I thought would be a simple task, became something that was life transforming. I began to realize that I would quickly go through my Bible verses and my Bible study just so I could get to my iPhone and go on social media. As I began to realize that I once again was worshipping Facebook, I began to repent and ask God to take away that desire to be connected to the social media and He, as He always does, answered that prayer.

I began to transform in such a way that it was evident in my actions. It was evident in the words that I spoke. It was evident in my heart. I began to commit every single moment that I used to use searching social media to searching God's Word. There would be days that I could not go on Facebook because I had not looked through God's Word and spent sufficient time with Him. I recall one time going almost a week. On one hand I was thrilled that I could go that long without being on Facebook, but then what that told me was I went a week without having a deep personal talk and Bible study with God. That was unacceptable. So then again I tweaked my own personal behavioral plan and began to make sure that I carved out time daily.

I am not a person that watches television, so you would think it would be easy to carve out time. However, I'm always going, I'm always busy, I'm always involved in something, and therefore it was not as easy as what it would appear. Once I fixed my focus back on Jesus and was able to understand how, by utilizing those principles that I'm reading about every day, my life would run smoother, there would be more enjoyment, and there'd be more time for other things. It became so crystal clear.

As I journeyed through this process, I recall one day realizing that I'd made it to the other side. It was one afternoon where I was content with only being in God's Word with no need to search the threads of Facebook or Twitter or any other social media. I didn't have to rush through something in order to be somewhere. I was just content with what I had heard in God's Word. For me it meant increasing daily what was expected of my own Bible study, to the point where I would have to read an outside Bible study and comb through scripture and look at the expository statements about the scripture passage before I would allow myself to go on social media.

I'm happy to say, as I write this book, I still have the same behavioral plan for myself so many years later. Therefore, if you catch me on Facebook or Twitter, then you know that I have been sufficiently bathed in God's Word for that day.

As a parent, your children pay very close attention to the things that you worship and the things that you do. I never told my oldest daughter what I was doing with Facebook or any other social media. It had been about three months into my new journey and she asked why I didn't reply to something that was on Facebook. I began to share with her what God had put upon my heart and a new direction that I wanted to take. All throughout the next year I noticed a transformation in my daughter, where not only did she subscribe to the same plan that I did, but she even kicked it up a notch, where she would literally delete social media from her phone for weeks and months at a time in order to spend time with God. She told me that she did not want to even be distracted by the dings of notifications that would pop up on her phone.

I was so proud of the fact that I, as a mother, was able to pave a pathway that led her closer to Christ. It wasn't a long drawn out discussion about what I was doing and why I was doing it and she should do it as well. I only simply shared, this is what I have purposed in my heart to do, and why, and left it at that. As she watched the transformation come upon me as to how my speech may have been different, how my heart may have been different, how I responded to things differently, then she became encouraged to want the same thing. And now being a freshman in college years later she still subscribes to the exact same thing that she purposed in her heart several years ago. It is my hope that as she has followed this path, that my other children will grasp and take hold of this concept and do the exact same thing.

I am pleased to say that my twins have implemented the same type of strategy as well, at 13. I think for my twin son it's a little bit harder, as he has such a desire in his teenage years to be connected socially with his friends. I see, just as I did, he wants to rush through those times of study in order to get to the social media. I continue to encourage him to slow down, find God within all that he's doing, and then search out his friends after God's time.

A B C
ALPHABET SOUP

1. It is time to do a self-inventory. Where do you spend the majority of your time—leisure, social, recreation, whatever you call it. What are your focal points? Are they things that you can say are idols? Do you worship these things? If so, after your self-inventory set your eyes back on your Savior and understand how to worship Him.

2. Find ways that your entire family can worship God. I shared in the beginning of this chapter how our family loves to worship God in music. Maybe your family is not a musically focused family, maybe yours is more in speaking or in dance or in written poetry. Whatever your family can do together and worship, then that would be ideal.

3. Watch for patterns in your children's life that you may be able to help get their focal point back on Jesus. Do an inventory

with your children as well, as to the things that they spend the most time doing, and asking them to evaluate if there is an idol or worship of something or someone that's occurring.

Chapter X

X-RAY

1 SAMUEL 16:7—*But the LORD said to Samuel, "Do not consider his appearance or his height, for I have rejected him. The LORD does not look at the things people look at. People look at the outward appearance, but the LORD looks at the heart."*

I often wonder when I view television reports about young people committing heinous crimes, what is truly going on inside their heart. On the exterior we definitely see a hardened criminal that has committed acts of crime that may be unimaginable for some. I often wonder about the mother and the father, and how they may know their child's heart in a different way than the media. At times we will see the news media interview some of the family members of criminals. Often you'll hear them say this is so unlike my loved one, they were a good person, something must have happened to cause them to snap.

As I look at these news reports and I think about all of the things that we view externally, I often wonder what is in the heart of each of these individuals. For me to know that is impossible because only God knows what's truly inside the heart of an individual. Therefore, many times I am not quick to pass judgment or make comment because I too have been a fallen, and am a fallen person. Stories that I could tell you about my childhood would definitely have you question my heart. The thoughts that I may have had as a young person would not be the same thoughts that I would have as an older person. Oftentimes my parents will say in my adulthood, "I remember when you used to," and then fill in the blank. They will then comment that I am a totally different person than what I once was. They say that based upon my exterior change that they can visibly see with their eyes, not knowing all along that my heart had actually changed way before they were able to see the exterior change.

I wonder if that's true for many of our young people. Many of the children that we are raising may have a heart change long before the exterior has had time to catch up with them. And as parents, sometimes looking at that exterior, we judge prematurely. We may see a child that is struggling with being honest. We may see a child that lies repetitively. However, what we may not see is what God sees on the inside: That the child is trying, that they are committing themselves to praying regularly that God would take away a lying tongue, which is an abomination, away from them. And as they have prayed and committed themselves on that path, there may be events that test their new walk. And before we know it as a parent, we are condemning them for what we see as a lack of a heart change, where in fact their heart may have already changed and, again, the exterior may not have caught up with what we see.

I'm giving this as an explanation for us as parents to be cautious as we are dealing with change in our children, to not assume that God is absent within their hearts. We quickly rush to judgment based on what is occurring on the outside of our child. I am guilty of this just like many of you. I would assume that because I'm not seeing a quick outward change that I question what is going on within my child's heart. We as parents need to ensure that we exercise a "no judgment zone" within the home. We can tell our child about our disappointment in their repetitive behavior, but we should be cautious not to say that their heart hasn't changed. We can honestly say that your behavior does not resemble a changed heart. We can work with them to be in prayer that God is still working within their heart. Saying that is different than saying God is not working. We recognize that if our child has said that I'm praying and I'm trying to change and I'm asking God to be that change agent, that we are partnering with them to ask God to continue working in their heart.

We need to recognize that our children are going to be judged by their outward appearance by society on a repetitive basis. Being an African American mother, that statement holds such truth for me. I recognize that I have two beautiful African American boys that society may look at and not see as absolutely beautiful. In this racially charged society that we're in currently, most often we are seeing a fear of law enforcement as it relates to the exterior of our young African American boys. We need to be diligent in teaching our boys what the world may see is different than what God may see. It is unrealistic for us to think that our teaching would transcend into something that is a change agent in the midst of a racially charged society, but at least it's a first step that our children can begin to take to not live in fear if they are a minority that is targeted in any way.

I praise God for never judging me on what my exterior looks like. I am thankful that I have a Lord and Savior that loves me enough to take the time to wait upon my heart and to fashion my behavior to match what the inner workings look like. Just as patient as God has been with me, I would like to encourage every parent reading this book to be just as patient with their child.

The other day I was reading an email exchange from the elementary principal at my children's school. We were discussing an upcoming field trip which my fourth-grader and second-grader would be attending. In this email exchange I advised the elementary principal that because parents were not going on this trip due to limited seating on the charter bus, that my fourth grade son would look out for his second grade sister, and I explained that within our family our boys and our older children are taught to always look out for their younger siblings.

I loved the response that I received back from her because she said that watching our son Avery care for his younger sister Autumn reminds them of his tender heart. Why that was so important is that our son Avery, on the exterior, is 155 percent boy, always moving, always jumping, always running. He is a glorious picture of a rough and tough little boy. Therefore, his outward appearance looks rough and tough as a boy is fashioned to be, but in those moments where he is caring for others his heart exudes love. What a wonderful picture of God's Word in 1 Samuel, that man looks at the outside but God looks upon the heart. I praise God that this elementary principal was able to see clearly his heart the way God would see it.

How do you see your child's heart? Are you always paying attention to your child's behavior or have you begun to understand that there could be more happening within the child's heart? Clinically I recognize that when I'm in session with individuals, whether young or old, there may be a defense mechanism that comes out on the exterior. Because there may be deep feelings within a person's heart that they may feel they can't share for whatever reason, they may have this bravado on the outside that shields and truly hides their heart.

It brings to mind the Christmas story of Scrooge. Remember the whole concept of that beautiful story and how it unfolded? On the exterior you have this person who is hardened. But look at the heart change that happened on the inside that then eventually brought about an outside change. We don't know exactly how long it takes for the outside to catch up with the inside, but because God knows the heart of the person, God is the one guiding that process. We can take comfort in knowing that God will give us signs that He's working, that we'll begin to see fruit being born. We need to be fruit inspectors in the lives of our children. We need to see that if there is a heart change we will begin to see the fruit that's being born.

I want to be clear in saying that there's no contradiction to what I've said in the beginning of the chapter till now. We cannot 100 percent verify whether or not a heart change is taking place and how it's taking place, but what we can verify is that as the heart begins to change fruit is born, and because that fruit is born we will be fruit inspectors within the lives of our children.

We also will begin to see that when behavior alters and changes for the negative and we feel that our child's heart is not changing, that as long as we have been able to see fruit coming from the initial heart change we can rest assured that this is a trial that we can begin to pray with our child to help them navigate through. It could possibly be an attack from Satan, that as this child is changing and growing closer to God Satan wants that child. So we can begin to pray feverishly for our child that that doesn't happen.

A B C
ALPHABET SOUP

1. Begin to pray for your child's heart. Ask the Lord to show you areas in which their behavior has impacted the heart call and the heart change that God has started.

2. Have a discussion with your child about their heart. It is okay to confront your child about the inconsistencies in their behavior and what they feel their heart may be saying and how they feel their heart may be changing.

3. Put a plan together with your child on how you will be a fruit inspector in their life.

4. Encourage and teach your child to be a fruit inspector in their own life. Have them journal the challenges, the successes that they are having as their heart begins to change, and then changing their behavior.

Chapter Y

YOKED

2 CORINTHIANS 6:14a—*Do not be unequally yoked together with unbelievers.*

ost times we hear this Bible verse as it references individuals becoming married. We often will tell singles that they must find another believer in Christ and to not join into a union in which they are unequally yoked. As I ponder what this means in a marital situation, I wonder how the same concept would then apply to the friendships that our children have.

I remember a phrase most often used, "Birds of a feather flock together." My grandmother would always say this before she gave me a lecture about the type of friends that I had. I don't think that she really liked the group of friends that I had in high school because sometimes I would get in trouble staying out too late. Looking back, my high school friendships were some of the best friendships that I recall, but because we were a little on the rebellious side, according to standards in the 1980s, it caused my grandmother a great deal of concern.

The individuals that we associate with do truly impact who we are as individuals. The individual friends that our children have should be looked upon as possible influencers. Much like parents will get to know a possible mate for their daughter or son, I would suggest that parents do that also with friendships. There's absolutely nothing wrong with getting to know those people that will influence your children.

As our oldest daughter entered into middle school many years ago we began to see a change in her attitude over the sixth, seventh and eighth grade. At that time we decided to enroll her into a charter academy which was in a public setting. There were several types of families that were represented within the charter academy. The differences ranged from two-parent opposite sex households, to two-parent same sex households, to single parent households. With that wide of a variety of homes our daughter was exposed to many things that were never prevalent within our household.

Within months of being in middle school we began to see a change in her attitude and her behavior. Her once jovial spirit and joyous laughter that was always prevalent between her and her father started to change to a scowling look at her dad and a lack of respect. How quickly this little girl could change overnight. We began to pray and ask God for guidance in where we could help our daughter navigate back to a path that would be pleasing to Him. We would make strides, but the strides would be small and then we would take steps backwards. There was never anything horrid that happened within those three years of middle school; however, there was a definite dissonance in the relationship that she shared with her father that was once so close. At one point I thought maybe this was a transition that most girls go through as they deal with growing older as a young woman, then I realized that this was not the case. I realized that all through her young childhood there had been this human reverence for her father, that he was the person that she could turn to, like mommy, in times of trouble and could confide her heart's most precious issues.

As we dug deeper and began to truly examine the type of friendships that our daughter had at the time, we recognized a pattern. The pattern was that all of her friends that were females had terrible relationships with their fathers. They would say negative things about their fathers in the presence of each other, to the point where our daughter didn't have anything negative to say but she would feel negativity towards him based on how her friends felt. Never underestimate the power of influence that your children's friends can have over them. Even though it did not have irreparable damage, and I praise God for that, we can tell that there was a definite shift in how that relationship evolved in that three-year period.

As God began to open our eyes and allow us to see exactly what was occurring we made the decision, for high school, to move our daughter to a Christian academy. We were pleased to find Washtenaw Christian Academy, where she spent the next four years. We did not know if making that type of decision would have an impact on the relationship between father and daughter. We were ecstatic and pleasantly pleased that within the first six months of being in ninth grade the relationship then again mirrored everything that it was prior to middle school.

I am not passing judgment on a charter or public school versus a Christian school. All I know, for our family, is that a Christian education was vital and Christian education worked. It brings to mind the analogy of the three-legged stool, in that in order for there to be balance you have to have all three legs. We were able to finally have that last piece that allowed our daughter to grow spiritually at school, spiritually at home, and spiritually at church. Once she made that transition and began to have friends that were like-minded her relationship with her father changed.

She joined the basketball team her freshman year and I recall sitting at our kitchen table with several of the athletes from the basketball team. I was extremely surprised, and pleasantly so, to hear one of the girls talk about her family life. As they began to talk I happened to walk upstairs to my room. Out of eyesight but not earshot, I began to hear one of the girls say, "Oh, my father really aggravated me this morning." I began to cringe, thinking we just left this at the other school. As I turned to come back downstairs I heard the young girl say, "He wakes us up way too early to do Bible study. I love my dad, but it's aggravating to get up every morning for early Bible study." I absolutely chuckled at the top of the stairs, thinking if that's the worst complaint that someone has against their father then we must have made the right decision. It has been a blessing over the years to watch God solidify the hearts of our oldest daughter and her father back together again.

I cannot emphasize enough that this chapter in no way is to pass judgment on the type of educational system that you have decided to place your child within, but it is more an indication of the type of friendships and environment that your child is in. Prior to our children going out with any friend we must first get to know the family. We must get to know who the father and the mother are in order to understand the heart of the child. In order for our children to go on a play date, it is imperative for us to visit the home, see where they live and interact with all the family members. There's much to be said for observing the language that is spoken within a home. I don't mean actual language, but I mean the family dialogue that is spoken, whether or not it's an environment of encouragement or discouragement; is it an environment of help or an environment of being selfish. We pay close attention to all those dynamics. It doesn't mean that we don't allow our children to go into certain homes based on our assessment.

What it does mean is that it allows us to prepare our child for the type of friendships that they will have and help them navigate the ups and downs that may occur.

Do you know who your children's friends are? Do you know the people that they associate with at school? Do you know their friends on social media? Have you had a dialogue with them about the type of friendships that they have and how their friendships impact them? Do you know the stories that occur at school, at church, at play, at practice that involve your children's friends? Have you studied their friends? Have you been able to give input on the type of friendships that you believe God would have for your children?

What type of friend does your child need to foster a love for Christ? What type of friendship does your child need to foster a love for school, to foster a love for siblings, a love for mom and dad? Are the values aligned the same within the friendships that your children have?

If you begin to see a rebellious streak in your child or a disrespectful streak in your child, sometimes we need to turn and look at the type of friendships or the type of things that may be going on in your children's friends' household. Often our children are acting out in the same manner that their friends do and we could learn a lot by asking the questions about what's happening within each home.

Sometimes God allows this process of having differing friends in order for our children to appreciate true friendships. It's amazing how God allows us to be joined together with both believers and unbelievers so that we can begin the process of prayer. If there are friendships that your children struggle with because of a multitude of reasons, help your child to know how to pray for their friends. Begin the process of an active prayer life with your child in regard to the friendships that they have.

A B C
ALPHABET SOUP

1. Make a list of all the friends that your children have. For each name, ask yourself the following questions:
   - What do I know about this friend?
   - How does this friend influence my child?
   - Are there things that I may need to do to help encourage my child to have a better friendship?
2. Teach your child how to be a fried.
3. Have a dialogue with your child about the list that you created. Ask their input about how they see the friendship being a positive or negative influence upon them.
4. Lastly, commit all friendships to prayer.

Chapter Z

ZEAL

ROMANS 12:11—*Do not be slothful in zeal, be fervent in spirit, serve the Lord.*

As I think about this passage, my best friend Kenyatta comes to mind. In all things she does, she does with zeal. She has this amazing ability to turn any adversity into a wonderful thing that God has allowed her to walk through and she always does it with such a quiet spirit and a big smile. I have learned quite a lot from just watching her walk through life with zeal and zest and being fervent in spirit while serving God.

It is something that I don't see often as I walk into the grocery store or as I'm walking in the mall. I see a lot of individuals in these areas grumbling and mumbling. There seems to be a constant scowl that comes across the face or the brow of many people in society. There seems to always be a problem. There seems to always be a reason why we have to frown and we can't be happy and we can't live life the way that God has intended it to be.

What does the word "zeal" actually mean? The word zeal is defined as great energy or enthusiasm in pursuit of a cause or an objective. So as we look at God's Word in Romans, isn't it amazing that God would tell us to have zeal? He's instructing us to not be slothful in zeal. He's saying to us that there are certain behaviors and characteristics of a Christian and this is one of them. You want to have great energy and you want to be able to have great enthusiasm. And what is that pursuit? That pursuit is the continual walk and relationship that you have with Christ Jesus. It's amazing that God plans out this life in such a way that we're able to walk through it with zeal.

I understand completely as you're reading these words you may be saying, you don't understand the trial that I'm in right now. You may be saying, you don't understand the husband that I'm married to, you don't understand the trials that I have with my children and the agony that I've had with my job, or the frustrations that I have with my church; you just don't understand. And you're right, I may not understand, but God does. I know that His Word is prescriptive. His Word is prescriptive in that He knows every single thing about your life, but yet He still tells us not to be slothful in zeal. By telling us not to be slothful in zeal, He is giving us an amazing gift that reminds us that as we walk through life, we are to be walking through it in a way that is pleasing to Him.

One of my favorite pictures that I saw online was a person standing in a hallway with many doors closed and the caption said: Dear God, as I wait for you to open a door can I praise you in the hallway? I absolutely love that because it speaks to where we are as a society. We may see God close a door and immediately have several reactions. We may get angry, we may be frustrated, or we may go into a deep depression because we've placed our all in a door that we thought we should walk through. But in some cases God closes multiple doors. He closes them sometimes one at a time, or sometimes all at once. But instead of falling into a pity party or depression, God's Word is sharing with us that if we are not slothful in zeal we should be praising Him in the hallway because there's an expectancy that whatever God has for us, is for us, and nobody else is going to have it.

Don't misunderstand. I'm not stating a name-it-and-claim-it type of philosophy. What I'm saying is that God has something that is just for you and as He brings you through whatever trial, you should continue to dance and jump and praise Him while you're waiting. That is the zeal that He wants you to have.

So how do you show that type of zeal to your children? How do your children walk through life with zeal? Very simple: They watch you and they imitate you.

I most often will speak with children in counseling for a few weeks before calling their parents into the session. It is very interesting that by the time their parents come into the session that I already know who they are based on the complaints, concerns, attitudes and behaviors that their child exhibits. Most often they imitate and emulate the exact same ways and behaviors the parent has.

I can always tell when my children come home from school and discuss classmates, which children have parents that have zeal, versus which parents have a gossiping heart, versus which parents have a rumoring heart, a bitter heart. It comes out in their children. The children will utter their parent's language about certain topics that show the heart of their parent. So if you want your child to understand what God's Word truly means in Romans 12:11 about having zeal, you need to exhibit that first. Your child needs to see you happy when God closes a door.

One of my favorite passages is James 1:2, where God says count it all joy when you fall into various trials. I have to tell you it took me a while to be excited about that verse, but then I began to realize that

God is telling me that trials are going to happen. There's nothing I can do to avoid them, but what He tells me to do is count it all joy. And because I know He loves me and because I know that He is my loving Savior there must be a reason that He's telling me to count it all joy, and I don't believe it's because He wants me to be miserable. I truly believe that He wants me to count it all joy because there's going to be a change that will come about as I am able to accept whatever it is that He gives to me, good or bad.

It is exciting to be able to say that in the midst of counting it all joy, God blessed. In the midst of having zeal, God blessed. No matter what the circumstance is I can have zeal, I can have joy, because I know who my Father is. Regardless if God never does another thing for me, because He saved me I have the most grateful heart there is to want to serve Him in everything. Regardless if I never see anything that I want in my lifetime that I deem as important, I have salvation. I have the most important thing that matters.

It may seem contrite or Christianese to say those words and to read them on paper, but this place that I'm in now came after many years of pain, ups and downs, and literally God hitting me over the head with a neon sign saying, look at My Word. But after all of that, the zeal and zest that I have for life now is amazing. And I see my children being able to have that same type of zest and zeal. It brings me joy.

What are you excited about as a parent? Where is your zest, where is your zeal as a parent? How do you portray that to your child? How do you handle a crisis? Do you fall apart and begin to curse the world? When there's a trial that happens, do you begin to curse at the person who has wronged you? It could be something as simple as what happens when a waiter or waitress brings you the wrong food; how do you handle that? Is there still a compassion and zeal for life that you exhibit and show your child? How do you exercise forgiveness in front of your children, and compassion, that still maintains that zest and zeal that God would have you as a believer to have?

A B C
ALPHABET SOUP

1. Check your zeal. Are you excited about life? Are you excited about the things that God has in store for you? How do you as a parent handle the trials and tribulations that come your way?

2. How do you manifest that to your children? Talk to your children about zest and zeal for life. Talk to them about what God's Word speaks of in Romans 12 and how they can have a new take, a new zeal on life.

CONCLUSION

I will end the book the way I started: There is absolutely no way that any of the principles in this book can be implemented without a personal relationship with Jesus Christ. Salvation has to be the first thing that your family focuses upon. Joshua 24:15 says, "As for me and my house, we shall serve the Lord." As a parent, I implore you to search God's Word to first and foremost ensure that your household is saved.

I walked you through how to make that happen in the introduction, how to take the Romans Road and do a self-check, and then take a moment and accept Christ as your personal Lord and Savior. There is no better gift that you can have for yourself, and there's no greater gift that you can give to your children. You may not be the one to lead your child to Christ; however, you are the one to have a house that is a fertile ground for the seeds that are planted to grow.

In order for your child to understand any of the principles in this book that you may implement, they have to understand that everything that you do is consistently backed up by God's Word because of who you are in Christ. Your children do not have to be saved for you to read this book. You can pray for them through every single chapter and ensure that at the end of every chapter you're praying for their salvation. Continue to pray for them.

This book will be a guide for you to lay down that foundation, that fertile soil; that as you are cultivating the seeds that have been sown within that fertile ground you will be able to see the fruit that is born.

I pray that this book will be considered a timeless tool that will help your family grow in their faith. I also pray that reading this book encourages you to share with others the fruit that has been born from your life experiences. So many trials, so many successes have come throughout my lifetime, and I realize that God does not want me to keep those to myself, but instead He encourages me to share with others.

Therefore, I leave you with this: As you grow and learn from this book please share, not just the book, but the principles within the book that may help others grow as well. Together we can all go against the grain and raise Christ-focused children.

NOTES

CHAPTER B

1. Guinness World Records, *Guinness World Records 2016* (Vancouver, B.C.: Jim Pattison Group, 2015).

CHAPTER F

1. *"The Fatherless Generation,"* IDS 302 Project, April 23, 2010, https://thefatherlessgeneration.wordpress.com/statistics/

CHAPTER H

1. Tony Evans, *God's Portrait of a Kingdom Family* (eBook offered by The Urban Alternative, 2014) http://go.tonyevans.org/christian-free-ebook-gods-portrait-of-a-kingdom-family

1. CHAPTER R

Hicks, Jr., Maurice. *LeVar.* Uncle Reese. © 2014 by Hicks Music, LLC, Obed Music Group. B00K9JSS3I. CD.